laon

soissons

argenteuil
PARIS
st. denis
châlons

corbeil
provins

chartres
étampes
melun
paraclete
troyes

sens

burgundy

châlon

paray-le-monial
cluny

marcigny

lyons

DATE DUE

SEP 2 7 2006			

#47-0108 Peel Off Pressure Sensitive

HÉLOÏSE

by

ELIZABETH HAMILTON

Garden City, New York

DOUBLEDAY & COMPANY, INC.

1967

Library of Congress Catalog Card Number 67–10380
Copyright © 1966 by Elizabeth Hamilton
All Rights Reserved
Printed in the United States of America
First Edition in the United States of America

Non quaerit quae sua sunt.

[(Love) seeketh not her own.]

I Corinth. xiii, 5.
Quoted by Abelard in a dissertation
on the nature of love, *Expositio in
Epist. Pauli ad Romanos*, P.L. c. 891.

*Nihil unquam (Deus scit) in te nisi te requisivi; te pure, non tua
concupiscens.*

[Nothing, God is my witness, have I ever sought in you other than
yourself. You alone and not what was yours have I desired.]

Héloïse writing to Abelard.
P.L. Ep. ii, 184.

PRELUDE

It happened a long time ago. I cannot have been more than sixteen. Yet I see it all as though it were before my eyes. It was the end of afternoon school, the classroom almost empty.

"Come on," I said, "do come."

Then, as she made no move, I went across the room and glancing over her shoulder at the book open on the desk in front of her I read:

Eloïsa to Abelard

by

Alexander Pope

Impatience gave way to curiosity. "Who," I asked, "is Eloisa?"

She went on reading. In the silence a bumble bee blundered in through the window, collided with some irises on the mantelshelf, then blundered out.

"Who," I repeated, "is Eloisa?"

She turned her head—her hair was dark and silky, her lashes dark against the pallor of her cheek.

"Eloisa?" she said. "Why, Héloïse who loved Abelard."

Still at a loss, I asked: "And did Abelard love her?"

There was a moment of hesitation. And then she replied: "Yes, he did—in his own way."

ACKNOWLEDGEMENTS

I would like to thank all those who in one way or another have helped me in the writing of this book. I wish to express my particular gratitude to the Reverend Fr. Anselm, O.D.C., Carmelite Priory, Kensington, for clarifying points of mediaeval Canon Law; to Dom Gérard, O.S.B., Abbaye Saint-Pierre, Solesmes, for advice concerning visits to Benedictine abbeys in France; to Mr. Kevin O'Rawe for the chronology, map, and the loan of books on mediaeval Paris; to Mrs. Hertha Orgler, colleague of the late Dr. Alfred Adler, for discussions on points of psychology; to Les Sœurs de la Charité de Saint-Louis at Saint-Gildas-de-Rhuys, and Les Sœurs de Saint-Joseph de Cluny at Saint-Marcel, Chalon-sur-Saône, for help in both these places; and to M. le Baron and Mme. la Baronne Walckenaer for their kindness and hospitality at the Château du Paraclet, Nogent-sur-Seine.

E. H.

CONTENTS

HÉLOÏSE

CHAPTER I

Adolescentula quaedam nomine Heloisa.
[A young girl whose name was Héloïse.]

Abelard. *Hist. Calam.* P.L. 126

Now there was living in the city of Paris a young girl whose name was Héloïse": *Erat quippe in ipsa civitate Parisiensi adolescentula quaedam nomine Heloisa.* These words from the *Historia Calamitatum,*[1] an essay in autobiography written by Peter Abelard in the first half of the twelfth century, have in the Latin a haunting freshness. They steal upon the ear as might a gentle melody heard among savage chords. Or like a spell they work on the imagination, inviting the reader to attend to a story that waits within a story to enfold itself.

They were in my mind one morning in the late summer of 1963 as I stood in the shadow of Notre-Dame, where the rue du Cloître runs the length of the cathedral's north side. Crossing the street I turned into the curving rue Chanoinesse, leaving behind the excited nasal voices of a party of Italians crowding out of a motor-coach. I was in the area that extending north-east from the cathedral, in the direction of the river, comprised in mediaeval times the cloister of Notre-Dame. It was not a cloister in the monastic sense, but more in the nature of a close containing separate houses (some of them had gardens) inhabited by members of the chapter—the whole being enclosed by a wall with its own entrance. One thinks perhaps of a close in some English cathedral city. Vicars' Close at Wells in Somerset is particularly apposite—the small houses, the gardens, the high walls, the arched gate-

way; the drowsy quiet, as though time down the centuries
had stood still, broken by little else than the chimes of the
clock or the clang of a bell. But in the eleven hundreds the
cloister of Notre-Dame was not a place of quiet. Adjoining it,
if not actually in it, was the cloister school that was rapidly
becoming the centre of the intellectual life not only of Paris
but of Europe. The narrow unpaved streets rang with voices
of scholars and students, disputing the philosophical issues of
the day—the implications of Nominalism and Realism, the
significance of Universals.[2] They came in thousands, athirst
for argument and knowledge, from all parts of France, from
Flanders, England, Ireland, Spain, Rome. Foulques, prior of
Deuil, writing to Abelard reminds him how, during the years
when the latter was master of the cloister school, nothing
could stand in the way of these students—not distance nor
mountains nor valleys nor the sea. Nor was this due solely
to the magnetism of Abelard's personality. It was the spirit
of an age that intellectually was being born anew, one that
was a renaissance in its own right, that could not have enough
of asking questions. Moreover, it required that the replies
should be based on reasoned argument. And this was something that had begun in the previous century, when worried
young men had come to Saint Anselm, asking for a rational
exposition of the dogmas of Christianity. It was said of the
saint that many came to ask questions and, having come,
stayed because the answers he gave were convincing.

At a house which a plaque indicates as having been the
home of Pierre Trimouillat, *chansonnier humoriste,* I turned
to the right out of the rue Chanoinesse into what was scarcely
more than a passage closed in on either side by high walls.
I was in the rue des Chantres, the street of the choristers.
Did its silence belie the name? Or was it rather a silence that
held within itself the voices of past centuries, containing
them like a flower contained within glass? So deep was the

quiet that a footstep echoed in isolation and the voice of a child hung suspended like blossom on the wind. The strip of sky overhead was a blue so intense that I had the illusion of being in some city of the south. Avignon perhaps. I thought how at nightfall this vivid, sparkling blue would give place to a cool mysterious darkness lit with glinting stars—starlight above shadowy, labyrinthine streets. The words of Baudelaire came to me: *O nuit, ô rafraîchissantes ténèbres! . . . dans les labyrinthes pierreux d'une capitale, scintillement des étoiles.*

Passing on the left a narrow pointed window, then a nail-studded door—both of them mediaeval in character but part of a reconstruction belonging to our own day—I came out into sunlight at a juncture with the rue des Ursins. Here a flight of steps went up to the quai aux Fleurs. To the right, where the latter formed an angle with the rue des Chantres, a pair of adjoining houses—tall, rather faded, with shuttered windows—looked on to the Seine, separated from it by the width of the road and then a wall. Above the door of each house were stone medallions representing in high relief, in the romantic tradition of the seventeen hundreds, one the head of a woman, the other that of a man. A plaque common to the two houses bore the words:

Ancienne Habitation d'Héloïse et d'Abélard
1118
Rebatie 1849

The houses, numbers 11 and 9 of the quai aux Fleurs (this is the order if one approaches in the way I have described), occupy the site where—until the widespread demolition that took place on the Ile de la Cité in 1849—there had stood the house in which, according to tradition, Héloïse had lived with Fulbert her uncle, a canon of Notre-Dame; where, moreover, Abelard came to live in the capacity of tutor to Héloïse. In

those times it was the last house on the right as one came
along the rue des Chantres from the direction of Notre-
Dame. The quai aux Fleurs not yet having come into existence, the ground dropped to where boats put in at the little
Port Saint-Landry, named after the bishop of Paris who
founded the Hôtel-Dieu. That the house in question was in
fact that of Fulbert there is no irrefutable proof. Yet, as
Charles de Rémusat the nineteenth-century biographer of
Abelard has said, this tradition is in itself evidence: *cette tradition a valeur par elle-même.* Moreover, the position is in
accord with the pretext given by Abelard for wanting to live
there—namely, that it was near the cloister school.

Héloïse is believed to have been born in Paris in the year
1100 or 1101. Some say that she was related by lawful kinship
on her father's side to the ancient and noble house of Montmorency. André Duchesne in his history of the Montmorency
family says nothing of this. He does however mention, as
contemporary with Héloïse, a certain Havoise de Montmorency who had a niece Adelvie or Aelvide. This may have
given rise to confusion. For the name Héloïse appears in
several forms: these include Heloysa, Heloyssa, Heloïs, Hel-
loïs, Helowys, Helwide, Helvuide, Helvisa, Helevis. Others
believe her to have been of humble parentage, basing their
assumption on the fact that she says, in a letter to Abelard,
that in loving her he had raised her above the great and noble
women of the day. But this need mean no more than that
there were women more exalted than herself—at court, for
example—whom Abelard, renowned philosopher as he was,
could have chosen in preference. A sixteenth-century historian, Papire Masson, says, but without giving the source of
his statement, that she was the natural daughter of a canon
of Paris called John. John could be a misnomer for Fulbert.
On the other hand, Abelard expressly says that Héloïse was
the niece of Fulbert. He uses of Fulbert the word *avunculus*,

which means a maternal uncle, as distinct from *pat*
uncle on the father's side. The word *avunculus* also o
an entry in the necrology of the convent of the Parac.
Nogent-sur-Seine, where Héloïse later became abbess—. necrology being a record of persons (along with the day of the
month on which each died) to be remembered in the prayers
of the community. The entry in question (it is for December
26th) runs: *Hubertus, canonicus, domine Heloise avunculus.*
[Hubert, canon and maternal uncle of the lady Héloïse.]
Hubertus could be a copyist's error for Fulbertus. Duchesne,
who mentions Héloïse as being a niece of Fulbert, a canon
of Paris, goes on to identify him with a Fulbert (a canon of
Paris in the reign of King Louis—that is, Louis VI who ruled
from 1108 to 1137) who, having acquired a bone from the
spine of Saint Ebrulbus, suffered scruples at possessing this
relic and made it over to a cleric to dispose of.

There is one mention of the mother of Héloïse. It is in
the necrology of the Paraclete for December 1st: *Hersindis,
mater domine Heloise abbatisse nostre.* [Hersinde mother of
Héloïse our lady abbess.] Whatever the truth as to the parentage of Héloïse, whether she was born in wedlock or out of
it; whether she was of noble or humble origin, her personality
as revealed in the story of herself and Abelard—her poise,
dignity and her intellectual qualities—suggests a background
of stability and culture.

We know from Abelard that Héloïse, before coming to
live with her uncle in Paris, was a pupil at the Benedictine
convent at Argenteuil, some six miles to the north-west of
the city and separated by a great loop of the river from the
abbey of Saint-Denis that was to play a significant role in her
own life as well as in that of Abelard. The wealthy and fash-
ionable convent of Notre-Dame d'Argenteuil went back to
the latter half of the seventh century. It was founded in the
reign of Clothair III by a nobleman Hermenricus and his wife

Numma and presented by them to the abbey of Saint-Denis
—though whether it was originally intended as a house for
men or for women is uncertain. Early in the ninth century
Charlemagne made it over to his daughter Theodrada, who
became prioress. After the death of Charlemagne it was laid
waste during the Norman invasions. Then at the end of the
tenth century Queen Adelaide, wife of Hugh Capet, restored
it, establishing nuns of the Benedictine Order and endowing
it with manor-houses, lands, vineyards and fishponds. Its
reputation for learning was comparable with that enjoyed in
mediaeval Germany by the convents of Gandersheim and
Landesberg.

The town grew up round the convent to which pilgrims
came in great numbers to see *la Sainte Tunique*. The story
of this tunic, which was almost as well known as the Shroud
of Turin, can be read today on the wall in the parish church
at Argenteuil. Said to have been woven for Christ by his
Mother and to have passed at the Crucifixion into the possession of the Roman soldiers or possibly of Pilate, it eventually came into the keeping of the eastern emperors. Irene,
empress of Constantinople, gave it to Charlemagne who in
turn gave it to his daughter Theodrada for the convent at
Argenteuil.

To me Argenteuil had meant the Impressionist painters.
The name brought to mind the railway-bridge over the river,
sailing boats, a sky mottled with clouds, lush grass, poplar-
trees or the flaring gold of autumn foliage reflected with a
hardly diminished brilliance in quiet water. I had fitted the
convent of Notre-Dame into this setting, gauging more or
less what it looked like from an ancient engraving which
shows it as situated on the north bank of the Seine, its solid,
spacious buildings, laid-out gardens and neatly planted trees
enclosed by a crenellated wall.

I was not prepared for an industrialised suburb, with chemical works, tenement flats, and, leading from the station, a road that takes its name from Karl Marx. And yet Héloïse is not forgotten. A wide dusty boulevard (lorries clatter along it) running more or less parallel with the river, bears her name. On this same boulevard a petrol-station and a clinic are called after her. The clinic and, at the back of this, a mediaeval ruin occupy the area where the convent once stood. Behind, the town reaches up from the river, its twisting cobbled streets, ancient houses, little shops that sell asparagus and peaches, seeming in danger of being squeezed out of existence by a mushroom growth of modern buildings. Looking back towards the river I was disappointed to find it blocked from view by electric-plant and other contraptions. I retraced my steps downhill, passing the clinic on the left. Crossing the boulevard I made my way through limes and chestnuts, the trees so close to one another that sometimes their branches touched. Between the trunks I caught glimpses of the river— a steel-grey, and then, in a sudden burst of sunlight, a sparkling blue. There was a flash of brass, and an ensign fluttering, as a barge slipped by. I came out of the trees to the water's edge. To the right was the bridge spanning the river; and in the distance hills. The sky was piled with great cumulus clouds that were mirrored in the stillness of the water. I remembered Baudelaire's stranger, *homme énigmatique*, who had no father nor mother to love, no family nor friends, only the clouds: "*J'aime les nuages . . . les nuages qui passent . . . là-bas . . . les merveilleux nuages!*"

In the early years of the twelfth century, when Héloïse, after leaving Argenteuil, was living with her uncle in the rue des Chantres, Paris had already begun to extend beyond the Ile de la Cité. On the north side of the island the Grand Pont went across to the mainland where there were churches and merchants' houses—these still forming part of the city and contained within its walls. To the south, where the Seine was the boundary, the Petit Pont led to the left bank on which, outside the city, were scattered dwelling-houses, abbeys and churches against a backcloth of fields and vineyards. In the main, however, the city was contained on the one island—where there is now the Ile Saint-Louis there were two islands, neither of them inhabited. And when Abelard says that Héloïse lived *in ipsa civitate Parisiensi* he means that she lived in the heart of Paris—on the island that was the cradle of the city and its focal point. Indeed all subsequent developments down the centuries have been to some degree an overflowing from the original island-settlement where Julius Caesar, in the year 57 B.C., harangued the chieftains of Gaul. On this same island in the reign of the emperor Tiberius, the *nautae*, or boatmen, of the Parisii set up an altar in honour of Jupiter. Fragments of this, unearthed from the choir of Notre-Dame in the year 1711, can be seen in Paris today, in the hall of the Roman baths under the Musée de Cluny. Rugged, simple carvings represent the gods of Rome and of Gaul: Vulcan and the twins Castor and Pollux; Esus the Gallic deity of summer; Keraunos, horned god of cattle. This altar may have been still standing in the sixth century when Childebert, son of Clovis (the same Clovis who, hearing the narrative of the Crucifixion, broke in: "If only I had been there with my Franks!"), built on the island the first church of Paris to be dedicated to Our Lady. The pagan altar was probably broken up by the Christians and incorporated into the foundations of the church. Childebert's Notre-Dame (the cathedral that Héloïse and Abelard knew) was in the same Romanesque style as the basilica raised by his father in honour of the Apostles Peter and Paul (it was later associated with Geneviève, patron saint of Paris), on the hill Lucotitius to the south of the city—now Mont Sainte-Geneviève. Notre-Dame was a simple, comparatively low building, long in proportion to its size (its length was a little over a hundred and thirty feet), and ending in a semicircular apse. One may suppose that it had round-arched windows on either side, and a triple porch. It occupied only roughly the position of the Gothic church we now see. Its walls were not parallel with those of the latter, the west front being tilted more in the direction of the present Hôtel-Dieu and the apse coming nearer to the river. Indeed, the apse would have come somewhere in the nave of the present church, and the portico well forward into the *parvis* or square in front.

By the end of the twelfth century the Romanesque cathedral had been pulled down to give place to the Gothic Notre-Dame. In the eighteen hundreds the old cloister area was demolished and with it the house of Fulbert. Saint Landry's Hôtel-Dieu, which had been close to the river on the southern side of the island, gave place to the pompous building that bears its name today. Later, with the construction of the road that runs along the quai aux Fleurs, the ground that dropped down to Port Saint-Landry was levelled. These are only a few of the changes that the Ile de la Cité has seen through the years. And yet it has retained its distinctive character, no less than does a woman despite changing fashions of dress or the ravages of time. Moreover, nature transcends the changes wrought by man. The radiance that hangs upon Paris today, shimmering upon stonework, bridges, and spires —that brightness of the atmosphere that is coupled with the pallor of limestone—is not new. Lutetia, the name by which Julius Caesar called the island-settlement, is believed to be associated with light, whether it be the clarity of the atmosphere or the whiteness of the soil. Strabo took over the name in the form Lucotocia. Julian the Apostate, who knew the city as Louchetia, marvelled at the brightness of the river— the clear water sliding under little wooden bridges; in winter, blocks of ice, like marble, and along the banks fig-trees protected from frost by straw. The river (such is the nature of a

river) has the effect of binding past to present, present to
past. It speaks of time and eternity; transience and perma-
nence. Heraclitus, the philosopher, used to say that a man
cannot step into the same river twice. And yet the river that
I watch sliding by today as I look across from the quai aux
Fleurs to the shabby elegant houses on the Ile Saint-Louis,
the river on the banks of which willows glow like tongues of
fire—this river is the same that was to Manet a wonder ever
renewed; that moved Verlaine to ecstasy, Baudelaire to a
brooding sadness; the same that Héloïse saw from her uncle's
house, carrying the boats into Port Saint-Landry.

Guido de Bazoches, a poet who was writing in the eleven
hundreds, says of Paris that she was "a queen among cities,
a moon among stars". He was thinking of intellectual pre-
eminence, for he goes on to say that on this island "philosophy has her royal and ancient seat". Already in the twelfth
century the city had begun to rival Rome in scholarship. It
had become, in Helen Waddell's words, "the *patria* of the
mind". This was the *milieu* in which the young Héloïse lived,
one in which—as has been the case in France to the present
day—women were not intellectually at a disadvantage. Héloïse had no need, as had Teresa of Avila in sixteenth-century
Spain, to hide her intelligence, assume in the company of
men the role of a foolish unlettered woman. Her qualities of
mind were acknowledged even before she met Abelard. Fulbert, though there is nothing to suggest that he was an intellectual, was proud of his niece, perhaps inordinately so. If
in deciding to have Abelard to teach her he was prompted
partly by vanity—by the distinction of having under his roof
the master of the schools of Paris, the most eminent philosopher of the day—there is no reason to question his sincerity
in endeavouring to make available for Héloïse the best possible education.

CHAPTER II

Primum domo una coniungimur postmodum animo.

[First united under one roof, we were soon one in heart.]

Abelard. *Hist. Calam.* P.L. 128

PETER ABELARD was born in Brittany in 1079 at Palais or Le Pallet, which is about twelve miles to the south-east of Nantes, on the road to Poitiers. The title Palatinus that was applied to him probably derives from his birthplace. His father Berengarius was a knight and landowner of some distinction, his mother was called Lucia. It is generally assumed that both were Bretons. On the other hand there is an epitaph which says that Abelard's father came from Poitiers, his mother from Brittany:

Namque oritur patre Pictavis et Britone matre.

Abelard writes of both parents with warmth, and of his mother with tenderness: *Carissima mihi mater mea Lucia.* [Lucia, my mother who was most dear to me.] Both parents, when their family was established, entered the religious life— a practice not unusual in the Middle Ages, but, in this instance, of particular significance in view of what later happened in Abelard's own life and in that of Héloïse. There is evidence that Abelard was the eldest of four brothers. One was called Radulphus, another (he was married) Dagobert; a third, Porcarius, became a canon of Nantes. There was one sister, Denyse. Berengarius was a soldier, but he was a man of intellectual interests. He gave particular pains to the education of Abelard, his favourite, who, after making exceptional strides in his studies, resolved not only to abandon the military career which he would naturally have followed, but also—that he might give himself wholeheartedly to learning—to relinquish to a younger brother the heritage and privileges that belong to the first-born: he left, he says, the court of Mars to take lessons at the knee of Minerva. But if Mars is the god of war, Minerva, as well as being goddess of wisdom, is the patroness of battle. And Abelard was a fighter. In deciding against a military career he was not withdrawing from the fight. Roaming from province to province of France in search of instruction and argument, simulating (as did the numerous *vagantes* who were his contemporaries) the peripatetic scholars and philosophers of ancient Greece, he disputed with his masters and having worsted each in turn went his way. Alert for every new idea, every fresh encounter, he had a volatile, mercurial temperament (*levis animo* is the phrase that he uses), which, along with a precocious genius, he attributes, at least in part, to his Breton origin. And he was probably right. For Brittany is a land precocious in blade and flower; and its wiry, dark-skinned men are as wayward as the wind-driven sea that breaks upon their coast. According to Otto of Freising, a contemporary of Abelard, Brittany had a reputation for clerics who, whatever their failings, had keen intellects (*acuta ingenia*) and a taste for the humanities.

Abelard studied first under the celebrated Nominalist philosopher Roscelin, whose teaching had been condemned at the council of Soissons in 1092, but who had been allowed to hold a scholastic post at the church of Mary of Loche which was either in Touraine or at Locminé, near Vannes, in Brittany. Having out-argued Roscelin, he left him contemptuously within a year. It may have been then (there is some uncertainty) that he went to Chartres, where he tried, with no great success, to master the rudiments of mathematics. In 1100 he came to Paris to the cloister school of Notre-Dame, where his master was the Realist philosopher, William

of Champeaux. In no time Abelard had made himself a burden to his teacher, arguing with him, refuting him, showing
himself superior in debate, to the annoyance not only of William but of the students who resented that a newcomer
younger than themselves should set himself above their master. Thereupon, in 1102, Abelard, presuming upon a talent
rare in one of his years, opened a school of his own to the
south of Paris at Melun, a town where the court was at that
time in residence. William was indignant; but since he was
himself in ill-favour with certain of the courtiers, his opposition served only to further Abelard's ends. So successful indeed was the latter that he presently transferred his school to
Corbeil, to be nearer Paris. Shortly afterwards, however, he
became ill "from overwork" and went home to Brittany,
where he remained, he says, for "a few years".

During the period between his coming to Paris in 1100 and
the year 1113, when he became master of the cloister school,
he was engaged in a more or less continuous warfare of logic-
chopping with the authorities in the world of philosophy.
First it had been Paris, then Melun, then Corbeil. Then, after
he had recovered from his illness, he was again in Paris where
his return proved spectacular. For finding that William of
Champeaux had withdrawn from Notre-Dame to the abbey
of Saint-Victor (where there is now the Jardin des Plantes),
he tracked him down, attended his course and disputed with
him afresh. According to his own version, Abelard's victory
over his teacher was complete, and he was invited in 1112 by
William's successor at Notre-Dame to take the place of the
latter as master of the cloister school. William, however, in-
tervened, nominating a third party, and Abelard set up his
school again at Melun.

But he was soon back at Paris. This time he established
himself outside the walls to the south of the city, on Mont
Sainte-Geneviève—lecturing to his students on the brow of

the hill (within a stone's throw of where the Panthéon is today), or possibly in the abbey of Sainte-Geneviève, the
twelfth-century tower of which still stands, rising above the
Lycée Henri-Quatre. He was only a few yards from the place
where the university of Paris was to be founded less than
a hundred years later. Indeed the student-life of the south
bank—the area that came to be called *le quartier latin* because Latin was the language of intellectual discourse—owes
its origin more to Abelard than to any other individual
teacher.

Abelard went home to Brittany for a second time (in the
year 1112), to see his mother who, after her husband had
taken vows in religion, made up her mind to do the same.
On his return to Paris he was, by virtue of his dialectic brilliance, to all intents and purposes master of the schools.[8] He
was in no hurry, however, to assume the position open to
him. Instead, he went to Laon to study theology under a
master called Anselm—not the saint of that name (he had
died as archbishop of Canterbury in 1109), but, according
to some authorities, a pupil of his. Some have said that
Abelard saw in theology an asset to his career; others,
that he was influenced by his mother's entry into religion.
At any rate, a mature philosopher of thirty-four he presented
himself among students years younger than he was. Four centuries later Ignatius Loyola was to do much the same—soldier
and man-of-the-world, in mid-life he took his place on a bench
among schoolboys. But whereas there was at times a disarming simplicity in Ignatius, there was nothing of the kind about
Abelard. As might be expected, he was soon disputing with
his teacher who, he says, was a fluent speaker, but one whose
words were devoid of reason. Anselm, according to his pupil,
was no better than a fire that fills a house with smoke instead
of lighting it with a blaze. He was like the barren fig-tree of

the Gospels; or the cumbersome oak cluttering a field of corn,
to which the poet Lucan compares the fallen Pompey:

> . . . *Stat magni nominis umbra*
> *Qualis frugifero quercus sublimis in agro.*

[He stands, the shadow of a great name, like an oak-tree
towering above a field of corn.]

Abelard was vain and intolerant. He was aggressive, too,
and ungenerous towards his opponents. But he was also a
man in many respects ahead of his century. Following in the
tradition of Saint Anselm, in so far as the saint favoured a
reasoned approach to religious dogma, he went further. Re-
nan saw in him the forerunner of the nineteenth-century rationalists. But Abelard was not a rationalist in the modern
sense. He did not reject the authority of the Church or in-
tend that his dialectic should contradict Christian revelation.
It was his purpose, he said, to support authority with "the
buttresses of reason". Indeed, he was a forerunner less of the
rationalists than of Saint Thomas Aquinas. God-given reason,
he held, should be used to its full, and doubt made to serve
God's purpose. Believing that constant questioning is the key
to wisdom, he was exasperated by what seemed to him the
cloudy eloquence of Anselm of Laon. Annoyed, too, by the
mockery directed against him by certain of his fellow students, he accepted a challenge to deliver a lecture on the
Scriptures, choosing as his subject an obscure passage from
the book of Ezekiel. His audience was a mere handful, yet he
made such an impression that his reputation was enhanced.
He was asked to give the lecture again, and then a third time.
The upshot was that Anselm, spurred on by two of his pupils,
Alberic of Rheims and Lotulf the Lombardian, suppressed
Abelard's course.

It mattered little to him. Success in the face of opposition

and scorn only confirmed him in the opinion that no intellectual attainment was beyond his capacity. Returning from
Laon to Paris, he was welcomed with acclaim. By general
consent, if not by formal appointment, he was master of the
school of Notre-Dame. "At that time," he writes, "I believed
myself to be the only philosopher in the world." He was
moreover, a cleric, but not a priest—Héloïse, in a passage that
has reference to a period a little later than this, uses of him
the words *clericus* and *canonicus*. A cleric (or clerk) in the
context of the twelfth century is one who is tonsured (the
tonsure being a symbol of continence) and whose rank is the
least in the ecclesiastical hierarchy—he has not necessarily
received even the lowest of minor Orders.[4] The word canon[5]
had two uses. It was applied to clerics (not monks) organised
into communities with the object of living more perfectly
than would otherwise be possible the *vita canonica*, a life,
conforming with the laws or canons of the Church—that is,
with the precepts of Christianity. The word was also used
rather loosely of clerics, whether in Orders or not, performing one function or another in a cathedral church or its
dependencies, but not necessarily belonging to the chapter.
It is in this sense that the term is probably applied to Abelard.
A canonry could have been attached to his position as head
of the school of Notre-Dame. The title would have conferred
on him a certain dignity, but nothing comparable to the prestige that the word carries today.

Up to this time, when he had now become master of the
schools and was esteeming himself mightily as a philosopher,
Abelard had led, he says, a life of chastity. The somewhat
closed intellectual life provided little contact either with
women of the nobility or with those less exalted. As to
prostitutes, the idea of them was repellent to him.

It was now, when he was at the peak of his intellectual

career (probably in the year 1116), that he first set eyes on Héloïse. He was thirty-six or thirty-seven; she cannot have been more than sixteen.

He saw in her, he says, all the qualities that are disposed to attract lovers. Her looks pleased him, and so did her intellectual gifts: "While in looks she was by no means inferior to other women, in literary excellence she surpassed them all": *cum per faciem non esset infima, per abundantiam litterarum erat suprema.* Abelard, who had to scale the heights, who had to be one better than his fellows—be endowed with that much more than they—would not (for sheer pride, if for no other reason) have been drawn to a woman who was not pleasing to look at. In saying that Héloïse was not inferior to other women in her looks he is saying a great deal. But that, in addition, she should be intelligent and learned— this set her apart. Her learning, he says, had made her known throughout France: *in toto regno.* And what Abelard says is supported by Peter the Venerable, abbot of Cluny. For the latter, looking back over the years to the time when Héloïse was a young girl in Paris and he himself about twenty-five years old, reminds her how he had admired her zealous pursuit of philosophy; and how she had surpassed, in learning, all women and most men. Moreover, for Abelard there was the further advantage that Héloïse could write, a rare accomplishment. This meant, he reflected, that it would be possible for them to correspond: to enjoy a pleasant interchange of ideas and express their thoughts with a greater boldness than would be seemly in speech.

Charles de Rémusat says of Abelard that a noble and secret instinct told him to love her who had no peer: *Un noble et secret instinct lui disait qu'il devait aimer celle qui n'avait point égal.* It was I think, not so much an instinct as a deep-seated need, of which Abelard was wholly unaware, to share his inner-self with one who was intellectually his equal (yet, being a woman, she was not his rival) and therefore able to appreciate his qualities of mind; one moreover who could give him the understanding and warmth necessary to his temperament—a warmth which his own aggressiveness kept at bay, turning into enemies those who should have been friends. As to there being an element of nobility in his choice of Héloïse, the choice (particularly when seen in the light of later events) can indeed be said to redound to his credit, but the manner in which he won her was base.

It is a story of calculated seduction, a campaign in which every contingency is coolly examined, every step planned. The fighter who had triumphed in so many conflicts saw no cause for diffidence; he was rich, he says, famous and good-looking. There is an unpleasing ring of complacency in his boast that he had no reason to fear a refusal, whoever the woman whom he might honour with his love. Awake to two traits in Fulbert's character, greed for money and an ambition to further his niece's education, he resolved to take advantage of these. Having therefore arranged an introduction through acquaintances, he contrived to be allowed to live in Fulbert's house, on the plea that it was near the cloister school, and that he was too busy to maintain an establishment of his own. In exchange for hospitality he was to be entrusted, in such time as remained from his students, with the education of Héloïse by day or night: he was to be at liberty to use corporal punishment if he thought fit.

So Héloïse and Abelard united under one roof were soon one in heart. Love rather than studies occupied their thoughts. Books were open, but the words that passed between them were of love rather than philosophy. Hands that should have been turning pages were busy with caresses. More kisses than ideas were exchanged. The pleasure they found in each other was the more intense, the more prolonged, because it was new to both. Abelard took to writing

love-poems which he set to music. The streets of Paris rang
with the name of Héloïse. Yet of these poems none has come
down (it is supposed that Abelard later, in bitterness of heart,
destroyed them)—unless it be that some survive in anonymity
among the scholars' lyrics that are the glory of the century.
The lover who offers a flower to his beloved—is it Abelard
speaking to Héloïse?

> *Suscipe, Flos, florem*
> *quia flos designat amorem;*
> *Illo de flore*
> *Nimio sum captus amore.*[6]

[Yourself a flower, receive this flower. For a flower speaks
of love. This flower tells you that my heart is yours.]

Héloïse, writing to Abelard years afterwards from the convent of the Paraclete, reminds him of his lyrics. He composed
them, she says, as a relaxation from philosophy. So lovely
were the words and the music that he won wide acclaim—
even simple, unlettered persons found pleasure in the tunes.
Something of the beauty of the language, the variety of the
verse-forms, can be imagined from his *Planctus*, six laments
on themes taken from the Old Testament, in which he who
formerly had taken up his lute for joy, does so now in sorrow:

> *Dolorum solatium,*
> *Laborum remedium,*
> *Mihi mea cithara,*
> *Nunc quo maior dolor est*
> *Iustiorque maeror est,*
> *Plus est necessaria.*

[I need my lute the more, my solace in grief, healing in
suffering, now that my pain is the more bitter, the cause of
my sorrow the greater.]

Abelard was occupied to the exclusion of all else with his new-found pleasures. Finding love-poems more to his taste than were the secrets of philosophy, he had no longer the inclination to prepare his lectures and contented himself with those he had used before. His students noticed the change and began to talk. Only Fulbert, it seems, remained blind and deaf—a fact that Abelard attributed in part to his own reputation for chastity, in part to Fulbert's love for his niece which allowed him to see no fault in her. "We do not," Abelard comments, "readily suspect evil in those whom we love. Nor in extreme affection, *in vehementi dilectione*, can the unworthy taint of suspicion find its way." Then, after quoting Saint Jerome to the effect that we are the last to discover the scandals in our own home, remaining ignorant of the vices of our children and wives, while our neighbours can talk of nothing else, he continues: "But what is last of all to be disclosed does, nevertheless, come to light in time; and what is common knowledge cannot be concealed easily from one person." In short, after some months had elapsed Fulbert learnt the truth and thereupon turned Abelard out of the house. "How great," Abelard writes, "was the distress of the lovers at being parted! What embarrassment and confusion I felt! What remorse for the misery I had brought upon this girl!" *Quanta contritione super afflictione puellae sum afflictus!* Each lamented the other's misfortune. Yet the effect of the separation was to make them reckless. Shame made them shameless, until, finally, they were surprised together as, in the myth, were Venus and Mars by Vulcan.

Shortly after this Héloïse wrote to Abelard, telling him that she was pregnant and asking him what she ought to do. She did not write in the manner of one who considered herself betrayed (it was not her nature to shift responsibility), but in "a transport of joy", *cum summa exultatione*. The words reveal the trust Héloïse had in Abelard—a confidence made possible only because she was certain that he loved her. At the outset Abelard had been guilty of the seduction of a young girl committed to his charge. He had betrayed her uncle who was also his host, mocking at the folly of this uncle in trusting his ewe-lamb into the wolf's keeping. But the lamb had prevailed over the wolf. Abelard had come to love Héloïse. In so far as was possible for one who was fundamentally egocentric, he had begun to think not only of himself, but of her. This had first been evident when he was turned out of the house by Fulbert. He had been on that occasion concerned not simply at his own discomfiture, but at the distress he had caused Héloïse. And now, when he heard that she was pregnant, accepting his responsibility for the child that was to be born, he took Héloïse into his own family.

Availing himself one night of the opportunity presented by Fulbert's absence, he removed Héloïse—having previously arranged to do this—from the house in the rue des Chantres, and either took her himself, or had her taken, disguised in the habit of a nun, to Brittany, to the home of his sister. The act speaks for itself. Had he regarded Héloïse as no more than the partner in a transitory love affair he would not have given her shelter among his own kinsfolk. His popularity as a teacher had brought him money and a wide circle of acquaintances. It is hard to believe that, had he so wished, he could not have found someone other than his sister to help Héloïse.

George Moore in his novel *Héloïse and Abélard* pictures the two as making the journey to Brittany together. They travel the first part of the way on horseback. Mortemer, Coudray, Etampes, Saint-Jean-de-Braie, Orléans. From Orléans they go by boat, by way of Meung, Beaugency and Blois, following the winding course of the Loire, between banks grey with willows, past sandbanks and islands, over blue water stirred by gentle puffs of wind. At Tours Abelard turns back to Paris, leaving Héloïse in the care of his sister and the sister's husband, with whom she continues on her way to Le Pallet. The route that George Moore describes is probably the correct one. That is all one can say. It is possible, too, that Abelard accompanied Héloïse. Their love affair was at its height at Passiontide: *in ipsis etiam diebus Dominicae Passionis*. He may, therefore, have taken advantage of the Easter recess at the schools to travel to Brittany. Or the journey could have taken place during the longer recess in the summer. But this can be no more than a surmise. His words *eam transmisi* are more likely to mean "I *sent* her" than "I accompanied her".

In Brittany, at the home of Abelard's sister, Héloïse gave birth to a son whom she named Astralabe.

It is assumed that Abelard's sister was the Dionysia or Denyse whose name appears in the necrology of the convent of the Paraclete in an entry for December 4th: *Dionysia, magistri nostri Petri germana*. [Denyse, sister of Peter, our master.] At the time that Héloïse came to Brittany, this sister was living either at Le Pallet or possibly at Clisson—perhaps she had moved to Clisson when she married. The fact that Abelard could turn to her points to a bond of sympathy between brother and sister. Apart from his students who, entranced by his quick mind, his dialectical brilliance, his ready wit and power of repartee, used to idolise him, Abelard had more enemies than friends among his own sex. Too often he saw men as rivals or as stumbling-blocks on his path to fame—enemies to be crushed or at least to be made look foolish. Where women were concerned the question of rivalry did not exist. Indeed his attitude to women is, in general, superior to that of many of his contemporaries. Reluctant to confer praise on his own sex (not once in the *Historia Ca-*

lamitatum does he acknowledge his debt to those who had taught him) for fear in doing so he might present others as superior to himself, he can be lyrical in his praise of women. In his theological writings and in his letters he takes instances, drawing in particular on the Bible, of women's devotion, fidelity, patience, courage, and tenderness. He dwells on the quiet courage of the women in the Gospels who, when the disciples have fled, remain steadfast throughout the Passion and the events that follow. It is evident that in women he looked for sympathy, warmth, protection—probably his mother and his sister had satisfied in him a need for these. Possibly, too, the intuitive faculty, more highly developed as a rule in women than in men, may have enabled women to discern more easily than could his own sex the diffidence—concealed under a mask of self-assurance—of one who, despite his boastings and his genuine attainments, likened himself to a man who having begun to build was unable to finish: *hic homo coepit aedificare et non potuit consummare.*

"There is nothing to see at Le Pallet," I was told in Nantes. "You should go on to Clisson." And in a sense, I suppose, there was nothing. The long straggling street had no particular character. The stone houses were ordinary. The few shops adequate, but that was all. The historical ruins were unspectacular. And yet I found Le Pallet charming—perhaps because it was unpretentious, unself-conscious. There were clusters of dark trees, a flashing river, farmsteads, cows grazing in small fields enclosed by high dark hedges. And yet the overall impression was one of space. The landscape reached away under an open, lonely sky. I might, I thought, have been in Ireland, were it not for the vineyards. They came up to the houses, their foliage a golden green above the red-brown earth. Vines were growing in gardens, too—flinging their tendrils over stone walls.

Beyond the last houses, where the road struck south-east on its way to Clisson and then on to Poitiers, the remains of a chapel dedicated to Saint Anne stood back beside a burial-ground ancient in origin but in use today. Beyond the chapel on the slope of a grassy hill called *la butte d'Abélard* were the turf-covered ruins of a castle, the home, according to tradition of Berengarius, father of Abelard. Above the ruins the hill tapered to a summit crowned by pine-trees and a calvary. Below, on the hill's further side, flowed the river Sanguèze, said to be named from the bloody frays between the Bretons and the Angles. The peace of the translucent water shadowed by willows, poplars and oaks, belied the savagery of the name. Cattle grazed knee-deep in meadow-grass. The warm air was laden with the sweet, elusive scents of the country-side.

As I retraced my steps down the hill, past yew-trees—their blue darkness accentuating the massed creamy white of elder-flowers, I met a peasant woman in black; her leather-brown face was crinkled, her feet shuffled in felt slippers. She looked hard at me. I could feel the silence between us. To break it I said: "*Abélard demeurait ici, je crois?*" Her faded eyes lit up. "*Mais oui, madame,*" she answered, and then she added in pride: "*Et Héloïse aussi.*"

On the road below, a funeral was approaching the burial-ground. An angular-looking white farmhorse was drawing the simple black hearse. Mourners in black followed on foot along the pale, dusty road. Sunlight silvered the poplar trees.

Le Pallet is unsophisticated, Clisson dramatic. At Clisson there are immense boulders, swift-rushing streams, gulleys, waterfalls, sombre ilex-trees, a luxuriance of mosses and ferns.

The ruined castle stands high above the confluence of the Maine and the Sèvre, its ramparts, on a clear day, mirrored in the green glass-smooth water carrying the ivory and deep-pink cups of water lilies. It was built in the early thirteenth century, about a hundred years after Héloïse visited Brittany, but in her day Clisson was already an important stronghold.

I had come there from Nantes in deluging rain. All the way in the bus rain had streamed down the window panes. There had been an occasional glimpse of wooded country—little hillocks and valleys, all intensely green. I walked through the almost deserted street, then to the left, past the imposing timbered market. At the entrance to the castle grounds the custodian looked at me pityingly as I handed him my fifty centimes—for the rain was still coming down: a grey, billowing curtain of rain through which the castle was hardly more than a pinkish blur. Presently the curtain parted. The sun, breaking through the clouds, shone upon great, rugged walls and towers, picking out, in the peculiar intensification of light following immediately upon rain, the surfaces of the stone, patches of lichen, and, growing in crevices, maiden-hair ferns and cranesbill. On the slopes of the fosse a black and white goat was cropping the drenched grass, its bell tinkling. Swifts tore the air in mad career. The wild, bewildering flight of the birds—this and their shrill cries gave to the scene an unreality. I crossed a drawbridge, then made my way up a crumbling stairway. The shell of the castle stood up about me. Overhead was the open sky and the swifts screaming. Through an arched window I looked down on to a great expanse of dark water, trees growing thick to the edge. It was no wonder, I thought, that the scene had so moved the romantic imagination of the young Lamartine that in the adjoining park of La Garenne he carved on the granite rock of a grotto, where tradition said Héloïse used to sit in reverie during the months in which she awaited the birth of her child, the following lines:

> *Héloïse peut-être erra sur ce rivage*
> *Quand, aux yeux des jaloux dérobant son séjour,*
> *Dans les murs du Pallet, elle vint mettre au jour*
> *Un fils, cher et malheureux gage*
> *De ses plaisirs furtifs et de son tendre amour.*
> *Peut-être, en ce réduit sauvage,*
> *Seule, plus d'une fois, elle vint soupirer,*
> *Et goûter librement la douceur de pleurer;*
> *Peut-être, sur ce roc assise,*
> *Elle rêvait à son malheur;*
> *J'y veux rêver aussi; j'y veux remplir mon cœur*
> *Du doux souvenir d'Héloïse*

[Héloïse perhaps wandered on this river-bank when, concealing herself from jealous eyes within the walls of Le Pallet she awaited the birth of her son—the dear, unhappy token of her secret pleasures and her tender love. Perhaps in this wild, desolate spot she came alone to sigh and taste unhampered the sweet relief of tears. Perhaps sitting on this rock she pondered on her ill fortune. I too would like to ponder here, to fill my heart with gentle thoughts of Héloïse.]

Wet or fine, by day or night, the atmosphere at Clisson is compelling. Above all is this so when the moon haunts the ruined castle; peering through a gaping window or staring down, full face, where once a roof hid the sky.

A link between Héloïse and Brittany is to be found in a folk-song called *Bazaz-Breiz*, published in 1839 in a French translation (along with a dialect version and the song's traditional tune) by Hersart de la Villemarqué who claimed that he had found twenty versions of the song in four Breton dialects. He was of the opinion that it went back, at least in part, to the life-time of Héloïse, and that incorporated into it were fragments of Druidic hymns of an earlier period. In it her youth and learning are stressed to the point of distortion.

The real Héloïse when she went to Brittany cannot have been more than eighteen. The girl in the folk-song, who travels to Nantes with her "beloved clerk", is twelve:

Je n'avais que douze ans quand . . . je suivis mon clerc,
   mon bien cher Abailard,
Quand j'allai à Nantes avec mon bien doux clerc . . .

Moreover, her learning takes her along the strange paths of magic. She is able not only to read and write; to speak Latin and the tongue of France—she knows all that there is to know in this world, all that has been and all that will be. She can find gold in ashes, silver in sand; turn herself into a raven, a will-o'-the-wisp, a dragon. She knows a song that has power to split the sky asunder, make the sea to tremble, the earth to quake. And, in all she does, Abelard is with her. If only they remain upon the earth two or three years longer, they will turn the world topsy-turvy:

nous ferons tourner çe monde à rebours.

CHAPTER III

Non denique meas voluptates aut voluntates, sed tuas, sicut ipse nosti, adimplere studui.

[It was not, assuredly, my own pleasures or wishes, as you yourself know, but yours that I sought to gratify.]

Héloïse writing to Abelard
P.L. Ep. ii, 184

Triste victime, obéissante et non résignée.

Charles de Rémusat, *Abélard.*

i

FULBERT'S fury, when he found that Héloïse was gone from his house, bordered on insanity. It had to be seen, Abelard says, to be believed. His first thought was of vengeance. But what could he do? Were he to kill or do injury to this interloper, this betrayer of his niece, retribution might fall on her, living as she now was among her lover's kinsfolk. Besides, Abelard was on his guard.

However, as time went on, so intense was Fulbert's distress, so extreme his anxiety for the niece on whom he doted, that Abelard could not but feel compassion and, as well as compassion, shame at his own treachery. In the hope of making amends he resolved to go in person to Fulbert—a decision that, in view of the danger to which he was exposing himself, must have called for no small degree of courage. Having, therefore, confronted Fulbert he admitted his fault and begged forgiveness. In doing so he adopted a line of argument whereby, while he stressed his own superiority, he minimised his responsibility. Since the beginning of time, great men, he pleaded, had been brought low by women. Moreover, to conciliate Fulbert beyond all that the latter could have hoped, *supra quam sperare poterat*, he professed himself ready to marry Héloïse on condition that the marriage should be kept secret, so that his reputation might not suffer. What precisely was in the mind of Abelard when he made this stipulation we do not know. Was it a temporary measure, until he could think out the future? Or was it a long-term one? Viewed from Fulbert's angle, the suggestion appears wholly unsatisfactory, since only a marriage that was public could establish the good name of Héloïse. One thing, however, is clear. In mentioning his reputation Abelard shows his concern as to how, if he marries, he will appear in the eyes of others. In short, his insistence upon secrecy must be related to the fact that he was a cleric (though not a priest) living in a society in which the marriage of the clergy, even when this was in accordance with Canon Law, was frowned upon as being in the nature of a compromise.

Fulbert formally agreed to Abelard's stipulation—and in so doing was supported by his friends. He went further. "The more effectively to betray me," Abelard writes, "he sealed the promise with a kiss."

Whereupon Abelard went to Brittany to bring back Héloïse, to make her his wife.

Abelard had decided upon the marriage without having consulted Héloïse. He had not taken into account her strength of will nor her independence: it had not occurred to him that she would hold a view contrary to his own. He was accordingly amazed, on reaching Brittany, at the opposition that confronted him. In the first place Héloïse feared, she told him, for his life. Nothing, she was convinced, would be able to placate her uncle: by no act of reparation would he be satisfied. She then took up the line of argument which Abe-

lard had used to Fulbert when stipulating that the marriage
should remain a secret—namely, that his reputation must not
be tarnished. Arguing from this with a vehemence that went
beyond that of Abelard, she insisted that there must not be a
marriage.

What glory, she asks, could be hers, since in marrying she
would be humiliating herself and him alike? What penalty
would she not deserve for having robbed the world of a light
of such brilliance? The marriage would be detrimental to the
Church. Philosophers would weep for shame. It were unfit-
ting, indeed deplorable, if he whom nature had created for all
mankind were to dedicate himself to one woman. Such a
marriage would of necessity be dishonourable and burdensome. Did not Paul say: "Art thou loosed from a wife? Seek
not a wife." But if Abelard would not listen to the Apostle,
let him pay heed to the philosophers. Saint Jerome, she reminds him, showed by a process of clear reasoning that a
wise man ought not to marry. Cicero (according to Saint
Jerome's account), when it was suggested to him that he
should re-marry—after his marriage with Terentia had been
dissolved—had replied that he could not attend both to a wife
and to books. In a passage that closely resembles in tone a
letter written by Saint Jerome to Eustochium, Héloïse argues
that domestic life is incompatible with the pursuit of philosophy. Who, while trying to concentrate on the Scriptures or
philosophy, could put up with wailing infants, crooning
nurses, chattering servants, or the grubbiness of small children? She is echoing the thought of Saint Jerome—but the
passage has a freshness, an immediacy, as though it were a
first-hand observation coming from Héloïse herself. Has she
in mind the household of Abelard's sister? Has she, during
her stay in Brittany, pictured Abelard the philosopher in such
surroundings, and dismissed the picture as unseemly? It is
well enough, she goes on, for the rich—they have spacious

houses that enable them to withdraw from the domestic scene. But philosophers are not rich.[7] Nor do the rich or those taken up with the affairs of the world give themselves to philosophy. That is why—so runs her argument—from the beginning of time philosophers, despising all else, have devoted themselves to the pursuit of philosophy alone. The greatest of these, Seneca, writes to Lucilius: "When you are at leisure, that is not the time for philosophy; we must neglect all else that we may devote ourselves to this for which no amount of time is enough." That is why, she continues, in every people, Gentiles, Jews, and Christians, certain men have set themselves apart, living lives of singular austerity and continence, winning for themselves greater glory by their manner of life than by their learning. If laymen and Gentiles have lived thus, bound by no profession of religion, how much more so ought he, Abelard, cleric and canon that he is. And if he cares nothing for the prerogative of cleric, let him at least maintain the dignity that is proper to the philosopher. If he is unmoved by reverence for God, then let the thought of his own honour put him to shame. Marriage, Saint Jerome pointed out, did not prove beneficial to Socrates.

The fundamental concern of Héloïse is not with practical objections to the marriage, but with an ideal—one which she knew would not cease to haunt Abelard. A philosopher born to serve mankind, a cleric who has given himself to the Church should not—this is the sum of her argument—bind himself to the obligations that belong to the married state. It is not a question of what is permitted. She does not say that the marriage would have been illicit. There is no reason to suppose it would have been. Abelard, as a simple cleric—that is the lowest rank in the ecclesiastical hierarchy—was permitted by Canon Law to marry. Nevertheless, his status as a married cleric would be ambivalent. Although the marriage would be licit and valid, to marry would, nevertheless, be to

exchange—in his view and in that of his contemporaries—a
higher way of life for a lower, a more perfect for a less perfect.
That is why Héloïse calls the marriage burdensome; and says
it would be dishonourable not only for him but for herself,
since she would be the cause of his fall from glory. Her argument must be seen in the light of an age in which the roles
of cleric and philosopher were inextricably linked. Even if
Abelard had rejected the ideal of the celibate philosopher as
extolled in the pre-Christian world—especially the pre-Christian world as seen through the eyes of Saint Jerome—there
still remained the fact that he was a cleric. Though clerics
were not necessarily philosophers, yet philosophers and those
who taught philosophy were, in an age in which learning was
hardly to be found outside the Church, almost invariably
clerics. What Héloïse was doing was to confront Abelard with
the ideal of the philosopher-cleric as set forward by himself
in his writings where he cites as his authority Saint Jerome
whom he calls "the greatest doctor of the Church" and "the
glory of the monastic life".

There are fashions in sanctity. A saint acceptable in one
place or age is not necessarily so in another. Saint Antony the
Hermit is not to everyone's taste. Nor for that matter is Saint
Thérèse of Lisieux. To many persons today Saint Jerome is a
remote somewhat crusty figure who quarrelled with bishops
and eventually withdrew to Bethlehem where he had a lion
to keep him company—and, to wait upon his needs, a following of devout Roman ladies. Today, those who acknowledge Saint Jerome as a Biblical scholar and are prepared to
rank his correspondence as being on an equal footing with
that of Cicero, are not likely to be seriously affected by his
views on marriage. In the twelfth century it was another matter. As Etienne Gilson has said, in whatever direction the
thoughts of Héloïse and Abelard move the vast shadow of
Saint Jerome precedes, follows, pursues: *Partout où leurs ré-*

flexions les conduisent Héloïse et Abélard sont précédés,
suivis, ou plutôt poursuivis par la grande ombre de Saint
Jérôme. In a period of intellectual revival in which men were
looking not only to the future, but to the heritage of Greece
and Rome, the writings of Saint Jerome—to whom the title
of saint was given in recognition of his scholarship (which
he put to the service of the Church) rather than of his
spirituality—provided a bridge that spanned the void separating the mediaeval world from a rich but hitherto somewhat
neglected past. A Christian, he was enmeshed in pre-Christian
thought. Of all the Fathers of the Church, he comes nearest,
in his handling of the Latin language, to the clarity and purity
of Cicero's style. He was steeped in Cicero and in Seneca.
Nevertheless, unlike Saint Thomas Aquinas who, six centuries later, could move gracefully between the classical and
Christian world, drawing on classical thought and terminol-
ogy to formulate Christian dogma, Saint Jerome was torn in
two directions. Hidden in the Biblical scholar was the poet
who admired Catullus with a passionate intensity. In one
breath he quotes lovingly from Virgil or Horace or Lucan, in
the next he decries the pagan poets as being "the food of
demons". And yet, protest as he will, he clings to these writers
and justifies himself for doing so, defending his constant
references to the classics with the plea that Paul quotes from
Menander and Aratus.

He betrays a similarly divided attitude in regard to women.
He had close friends among the aristocratic ladies of Rome,
notably Paula and Eustochium who accompanied him to
Bethlehem. Indeed, the greater part of his letters are addressed to women. In one he writes with tender concern to a
mother about the education of a little girl. Above all, the
child's lessons must be made pleasing to her and not distaste-
ful: she should be given an alphabet to play with, made of box-
wood or ivory. Her mother should teach her to write, guiding

her daughter's small hand with her own. The child must not be scolded but encouraged—since children work better if encouraged. He can write of family life with perception and understanding; and yet he presents marriage as at best a necessary evil, a state to be avoided if possible. In quoting (out of its context) Cicero's remark to Hirtius that he had not time for a wife and books, Jerome overlooks the fact that Cicero was a man deeply involved in family life, deeply attached to and dependent on the members of his family.

It was particularly in Seneca that Jerome[8] found grist for his mill. It was from Seneca that he borrowed the remark, taken originally from Theophrastus, to the effect that a wise man does not marry; because, whereas one can try out other things beforehand—a horse, for example—in the case of a wife this is not so. One would suppose, from reading Jerome, that Seneca had lived the life of a recluse, in extreme austerity, devoting himself to nothing else but philosophy. This picture does not conform with that given by Tacitus (whose writings were not available to Jerome) of a man so wealthy as to be embarrassed by his possessions; one moreover who, when he decided upon suicide because Nero required this of him, had the support of a wife who was prevented only by force from sharing her husband's death.

In the mind of Saint Jerome, Seneca was associated with Saint Paul. Jerome accepted as genuine the apocryphal correspondence purporting to have been exchanged between Seneca and the Apostle. In Paul's: "He who is unmarried is concerned with God's claim, whereas the married man is concerned with the world's claim, asking how he is to please his wife", Jerome finds a Christian counterpart to Seneca's injunction that the would-be philosopher must hold himself aloof from all else—whether honours, engagements, or marriage.

Not everyone in the Middle Ages had the attitude to marriage that emanated from Saint Jerome and from Saint Paul as interpreted by Jerome. The canonist Ivo of Chartres spoke of marriage as a "union between two souls". Robert de Sorbonne preached in a similar vein. Robert de Brun went so far as to say that there was no solace under heaven comparable to the love of a good woman. But Saint Jerome's voice spoke louder: to the twelfth century it might have been the voice of God. And Abelard, as is evident in his writings, had derived his views on marriage from Saint Jerome. It is no wonder, then, that Héloïse argued as she did. No wonder, that she resolved not to be a stumbling-block to Abelard's glory, not to bind him in chains from which there was no escape. What does perhaps appear odd, at least on a first reading, are the words that follow a train of argument that had been based largely on appeals to Saint Jerome and Saint Paul. For speaking now solely for herself, she says that she would choose to be Abelard's mistress rather than his wife; to hold him by tenderness, not by the fetters of matrimony; moreover, if they are separated for a time, the joys of finding each other again will be all the greater. Whereas she would rule out marriage, she will consent to fornication. Viewed from the standpoint of Christian morality this is strange reasoning—to argue against what is licit, then advocate what is illicit. It is on the part of Héloïse a last desperate (and subtle) attempt—intelligible, as much else in this story, only if related to the context of the period—to deter Abelard from the marriage. If he cannot do without her, then a liaison is preferable to marriage. As long as there is no marriage, he will be free (this is the implication) to revert to a life of continence—to find a place with Seneca and Jerome and their kind. That Héloïse, either now or in the future, would have put no obstacle in the way of Abelard, is proved by the pattern of her behaviour in events that have still to be recorded.

The arguments of Héloïse availed nothing. She could not

persuade Abelard. And so, against her judgement, she gave in, but with tears and forebodings. Years afterwards Abelard still remembered the words she had used: "Of a certainty we shall both be destroyed; and our sorrow match in its intensity the love that has been ours."

Why did Héloïse, having protested with such violence against the marriage, give in? Not because she was a vacillating character—in stating her case she had shown no weakness, no hesitancy. She gave in, Abelard says, because she could not bear to offend him. Indeed, she could hardly have done otherwise. For had she persisted in her refusal to become his wife, she would have appeared, despite all she might say to the contrary, not truly to have loved him. Besides, she was committed through the promise that Abelard had made to her uncle. Unless she agreed to marry, Abelard could not make good the pledge that he had given to Fulbert.

As Abelard continues his story a hush falls. His voice often assertive and braggart drops to a whisper. The very words he has chosen evoke quiet, caution, stealth. The participants in a drama heavy with mystery and pathos tiptoe across the stage. "And so entrusting our little son to the care of my sister (*nato itaque parvulo sorori meae commendato*) we returned to Paris unobserved. A few days later, after passing a night of prayer in a church we were married very early in the morning, in the presence of her uncle and a few of his friends and our own. Afterwards we went our separate ways, unobserved. From that time we saw each other only rarely and then in secret, hiding as far as possible what we had done." The Latin is besprinkled with words that suggest concealment. *Occulto. Nocte. Divisim. Raro. Latenter. Dissimulantes.* The name of the church is withheld—as though to give it, despite the passing of the years, would be to disclose a secret.

ii

Héloïse had returned to her uncle's home, Abelard to his lodgings, but their efforts to conceal what had occurred were in vain. Fulbert and his associates, despite the promise to the contrary, proceeded to divulge the marriage. Héloïse found herself in an impossible situation. If the marriage had to be disclosed, she was determined that she would have no part in the disclosure: as before, she felt bound to stand by Abelard's wishes. Besides, were she to admit to being his wife she could appear in his eyes to have been, after all, in league with her uncle—to have trapped Abelard into marrying her. Therefore like Hypermnestra of legend, who was forced into a falsehood that was more honourable than truth, Héloïse *splendide mendax*, proceeded in the face of her uncle's fury to deny on oath that the marriage had taken place: *anathematizare et iurare quia falsis simum esset*. Whereupon Fulbert heaped abuse on her—if indeed, he did not resort to violence: *crebris eam contumeliis afficiebat*.

Abelard learning of the maltreatment of Héloïse removed her to the convent at Argenteuil where as a child she had been a pupil. Before doing so, he put on her, he says, the garments of a religious—with the exception only of the veil.

That Abelard, knowing Héloïse to be harshly treated by Fulbert, should have chosen as her place of refuge the convent with which she had been familiar from childhood was reasonable. But why did he make her wear the religious habit? Was it already in his mind to make a nun of her? Those ready to think the worst of him have supposed that this was his intention—to rid himself of Héloïse: that it was only a matter of time before she would take the veil, the symbol of her profession. This, Abelard relates, was the view held by Fulbert: "Her uncle and his kinsmen, hearing what had happened, were of the opinion that I had tricked them and taken an easy way to rid myself of Héloïse by making her a nun." Certainly if Abelard had wished to create this impression, he could not have chosen a more obvious way. But the fact that he gives the interpretation as being Fulbert's suggests that the truth is to be found elsewhere. Besides, Héloïse, whose devotion to Abelard does not prevent her from analysing his motives with the same ruthless penetration that she applies to her own, gives no hint of appearing to believe that he wanted to be free of her. Thinking back over the years to this period, she speaks of herself and Abelard as being "separated for the time being", *ad tempus segregati*—he at Paris, herself at Argenteuil. As to the religious habit, Abelard, in requiring her to wear this, was without doubt putting himself in an unfavourable light. Those who saw or heard of her wearing the garment of a religious would conclude that she was intending to be professed. That they should think this would be to Abelard's advantage—or so he may have supposed—in that he wanted the marriage kept secret. If it was the intention of Héloïse to be a nun, then, after all, she was not, as Fulbert had declared, the wife of Abelard. She had spoken the truth, it would be concluded, in denying the marriage: it was Fulbert, not she, who was the liar. Abelard, angered at the marriage having been disclosed despite a pledge to the contrary, may well have derived a grim satisfaction in seeing Fulbert suppose that he had been foiled. What he did not take into account was the length to which Fulbert would go in retaliation.

The retaliation was swift in coming. Abelard records what happened. "And so, violently angry, they [Fulbert and his

kinsmen] made a conspiracy. One night when I was fast asleep
in an inner room at my lodgings they bribed my servant and
punished me by means of a most barbarous and shameful
vengeance—one that was heard of by all with utter amazement—namely they deprived me of that part of my body with
which I had committed the deeds of which they complained."

Abelard had, in the first instance, betrayed Fulbert. He had
seduced Fulbert's niece; and later, when she was pregnant,
secretly removed her from her uncle's home. He had stipulated with Fulbert that the marriage should be kept secret.
Finally, having married Héloïse, he had put her in a position
that, whatever the truth may have been, allowed it to appear
that he wanted to be rid of her. Fulbert had no reason to be
well-disposed towards Abelard. This much must be conceded.
Yet to do so is not to exculpate Fulbert. What had he been
about, at the outset, to leave his niece day and night alone in
the company of Abelard? And what sadistic streak in his character caused him to make a point of telling Abelard, should
he find his pupil negligent, to use corporal punishment? Even
allowing for the customs of the times, this injunction was
peculiarly uncalled for in the case of Héloïse who, from all
that is known of her, was plainly eager to learn. We are told
that Fulbert, because he loved his niece and was proud of
her, wanted to further her education. But was he thinking
primarily of her or of himself? Of himself, it appears: of the
prestige that would accrue to him from having her taught by
the most distinguished philosopher of the day, and from having this same philosopher living in his house. This, it seems,
blinded him to all else.

And the matter of the secret marriage? Granted that—in so
far as the good name of Héloïse is concerned—secrecy must
seem to defeat the purpose of the marriage, why did Fulbert
not only agree to secrecy but seal the agreement with a solemn

pledge, and then, as soon as the marriage had taken place, break his word?

And, finally, the vengeance. Why this particularly outrageous vengeance? It can be argued that it was dictated by frenzy against Abelard for his having, as Fulbert thought, rid himself of Héloïse by putting her into the convent. But even supposing Fulbert believed that Héloïse intended to be a nun, she was not yet professed—he could still have taken steps to bring her and Abelard together. However justifiably angry he might have been, one would have expected him, as the uncle of Héloïse, to put her welfare before all else. But he did the opposite. He once and for all wrecked the marriage. His action left his niece with a husband who was no husband. Further, he was publicising for future time the illegitimacy (at the time of the birth) of her child Astralabe who, if his parents had later decided to disclose the marriage, could (but for Fulbert's vengeance) have passed in the eyes of many as having been conceived in wedlock—whereas, now that the mutilation had followed hot upon the marriage, this was ruled out.

Some have thought that Fulbert had a further cause for indignation. Foulques, prior of Deuil, in a letter purporting to console Abelard after the mutilation, speaks of him as having squandered vast sums of money on prostitutes. If this was so, Fulbert had a double cause for anger—first, there was the insult to his niece; secondly (since he was, Abelard says, avaricious), the waste of money. But the value of Foulques' evidence is dubious, for he himself admits that its source is hearsay rather than fact. It could, indeed, have originated from a distorted version of Abelard's relations with Héloïse, whom Foulques does not mention. If, however, what Foulques says is true, this is likely to refer to the period after the marriage, when Héloïse was at Argenteuil—for Abelard, writing of the time before he had met her, says explicitly that he

had nothing to do with prostitutes; and he is unlikely to have
done so in the early days of their love. But if Foulques refers
to the period at Argenteuil, the evidence of Héloïse is against
him—and it is hard to believe that no rumours would have
reached her. Long afterwards her indignation against God
arises largely from the fact that the mutilation took place at
the very time when the two were living, she says, *chastely*—
she in the convent, Abelard directing the schools in Paris.
Moreover, Abelard, though he accuses himself of many weak-
nesses, does not accuse himself of this.

Héloïse, when arguing against the marriage, had shown
that she feared for Abelard's life. She had assured him that
Fulbert could not be appeased. She did not say merely that
her uncle could not be appeased by a secret marriage—she
swore there was no means whatever by which he could ever
be placated in this matter: *Iurabat illum nulla unquam satis-
factione super hoc placari posse.* What was in her mind?
What did she know that Abelard did not? The words that
Abelard uses in writing of Fulbert's affection for his niece are
significant. He describes it as being *immoderatus*—the same
word that he uses for his own love for Héloïse and she of her
love for him. It is sometimes assumed that Fulbert was eld-
erly. Helen Waddell in *The Wandering Scholars* refers to him
as an "old canon"; Octave Gréard in his translation of the
Historia Calamitatum uses the word *vieillard*, (*le vieillard
céda à la cupidité*) where the Latin has no more than *ille*
[that man]. In fact, there is no evidence as to Fulbert's age.
A fellow-canon of Abelard, he need have been no older than
Abelard himself who was in his late thirties. Certainly the
vengeance chosen suggests by its very nature less a wronged
guardian than a rival. There is no reason to suppose that the
affection Fulbert felt for Héloïse was in the first instance
other than that of an uncle for a niece, a guardian for a ward.
But when, in the warmth of Abelard's attentions, Héloïse

blossomed into maturity, did Fulbert's feelings undergo a change? Can it be—such a thing can happen in a flash—that, suddenly realising that Héloïse was no longer a child, he saw her as a woman who preferred Abelard to himself, and one whom Abelard had stolen treacherously from him to enjoy what he himself could not hope to enjoy?

Whatever motive lay behind the mutilation, for Abelard shame and humiliation far outweighed the pain of his wound, when, the following morning, crowds (he says the entire city —*tota civitas*) came thronging to his lodging, to lament, wail and condole. Where now, he asked himself, was the glory that a short while before had shone for him with a brilliance undimmed? And yet, he reflected, it was as he deserved; he was justly stricken, justly betrayed at the hands of one whom he had himself betrayed. How his rivals would gloat, his friends and family grieve! And the future—what did it hold? He would be pointed at by every finger, scarified by every tongue, a freak in the eyes of all. The texts of the Old Covenant, in which God rejects eunuchs, debarring them from his precincts, flooded his thoughts. The letter of the law might be obsolete, but the dishonour remained. And so, overwhelmed by shame and desiring a place of refuge—for these reasons, he says, rather than guided by a sense of religious vocation—he determined to withdraw from the world; to become a monk at the Benedictine Abbey of Saint-Denis.

Abelard did what he had set his mind on doing. He took his vows at Saint-Denis. And before he did so Héloïse had taken the veil at the convent of Notre-Dame at Argenteuil. "At my command" (*ad imperium nostrum*), he writes, "she took the veil of her own free will (*sponte*) and entered the cloister." The contradiction in his words is only an apparent one. She took the veil because Abelard had demanded it of her. Yet in doing so she acted of her free will—not, indeed, in entering the convent (there is no evidence that the religious life had the smallest attraction for her) but in submitting to Abelard's wish. Her friends did their best to dissuade her, compassionating with her youth and bidding her reflect on the rigours awaiting her. It was to no purpose. Her mind was made up. With a gesture of proud, defiant submission she went quickly to the altar (*ad altare mox properat*) and straightway taking from it the veil blessed by the bishop (*confestim ab episcopo benedictum velum ab altare tulit*) bound herself in the presence of all to the religious life. Her resolution had not wavered, but her tears fell. And from her lips there broke the words that the poet Lucan puts into the mouth of Cornelia, wife of Pompey:

> *O maxime coniunx!*
> *O thalamis indigne meis! hoc iuris habebat*
> *In tantum fortuna caput? Cur impia nupsi,*
> *Si miserum factura fui? Nunc accipe poenas,*
> *Sed quas sponte luam.*

[Noble husband—too noble for wedlock with me! Had fortune this power over your greatness? Why did I dare to marry you, if I was to make you unhappy? Accept forthwith the expiation that I shall offer of my own will.]

How far was Abelard entitled to ask this sacrifice of Héloïse? What was the position in the twelfth century as regards a married person who wanted to enter the cloister? The answer is not completely simple. Canon Law had not yet been codified as it was later, so that what applied in one decade did not necessarily do so in the next.

There are, however, two sources of information. First, the *Decretum* of Burchard, a work covering the entire field of ecclesiastical law, composed between 1008 and 1012 and enjoying prestige to the end of that century. Secondly, the *Decretum* of Ivo of Chartres, a systematic collection of texts taken from Burchard, Roman law, and contemporary civil law. The latter, which was intended for the practical use of the clergy, was completed by the year 1116, about three years before Héloïse and Abelard entered their religious houses.

Texts in Burchard and Ivo of Chartres established that, according to Canon Law, neither husband nor wife might become a religious without the consent, freely given, of the other. Burchard cites the instance of a certain Agathosa who complains that her husband has gone into a monastery against her will; if, on examination, what she says transpires to be true, the husband is to return to his wife. Ivo of Chartres quotes a synodal decree of Pope Eugenius to the effect that if a man and his wife agree to part with the intention of entering religion, this is not to be permitted without the bishop's knowledge, since, if either wife or husband is unwilling, the marriage must not be allowed to be broken up. Again, in the case of a man who wishes to separate from his wife for this same reason, Pope Nicholas is quoted as writing to the bishops of Britain saying that it is permissible only with the consent of both parties: *ex consensu ambarum partium*. A text of particular significance given by Ivo of Chartres translates: "If some persons say that for the sake of the religious life marriages ought to be dissolved, it must be known that, even if human law has permitted this, the divine law has none the less forbidden it. If indeed the wife does not consent to the life of continence desired by the husband or if the husband rejects that desired by the wife, the marriage may not be sundered."

It is plain from the texts that, assuming the husband or wife has had his or her partner's consent to enter religion, the latter is required to do the same or, if not to enter religion, to take a vow of chastity in the world. Burchard cites the case of a man who, having given permission to his wife to take the veil, is told that he is to adopt a like way of life:

similiter convertatur. He also quotes Bishop Basil as saying: "If a married man wants to enter a monastery he is not to be accepted unless he has first been made free to do so by his wife's taking a vow of chastity". Of particular relevance because cited not only by Burchard, but also by Ivo and therefore close in time to Héloïse and Abelard, is a letter addressed by Pope Nicholas I to King Charles the Bald, in which he says that he has written to Queen Theutberga, wife of Lotharius, who had asked that she might renounce her royal prerogative and live privately in chastity, to the effect that this is not possible unless her husband shall choose a like manner of life. The texts suggest that it was usual when a husband or wife entered religion for the partner to do the same, but this was not necessarily so, provided a vow of chastity was taken. Abelard, writing of his mother Lucia, says that after her husband had entered religion she "was minded (or 'arranging') to do the same": *idem facere disponebat.* The words do not imply compulsion, but rather that, had she wished, she could have remained in the world. This occurred about 1112. There is no reason to suppose that the same could not have held good for Héloïse some eight years later.

Abelard says that Héloïse took the veil at his command. In fact, he was in no position to give any such command. His doing so becomes the more ridiculous when one reflects that his own entry into Saint-Denis was dependent upon the consent of Héloïse, his wife. And she, prompt though she was to carry out his wishes, knew this. Possibly it was in her mind when later, giving her version of how she came to take the veil, she substitutes for Abelard's authoritative *imperium* (command), the less forcible word, *iussio* (bidding). "It was not a sense of vocation, but your bidding that induced me to face the austerities of the religious life." Héloïse obeyed Abelard not because she had to, but for reasons of her own. Her obedience was neither then, nor on any other occasion, that of a slave. It was a deliberate, willing submission.

Abelard ordered Héloïse to take the veil not because he had the right to do so, but because he was the person that he was. But what were his motives? For whereas he has given his reasons for his withdrawal to Saint-Denis—a sense of shame coupled with a desire for a place of refuge—he says nothing of the decision that he made regarding Héloïse. A number of motives suggest themselves, one not necessarily excluding the other. Was it, in part, vengeance against Fulbert—a determination to do the very thing (that is, rid himself of Héloïse by enclosing her in a convent) that Fulbert had formerly suspected him of doing? On the emotional level this is intelligible. But, in fact, this vengeance, if such it was, had become purposeless, since, now that Fulbert and Héloïse were, as a result of the mutilation, irreparably alienated, it could have mattered little to her uncle whether she was in a convent or out of it. Again, was there in Abelard's mind an intention (now that he saw no life possible for him other than that of the monastery) to provide for Héloïse—to protect her from the dangers and difficulties, physical, moral, and possibly financial, that could attend a young girl, debarred the shelter of her uncle's home, living the life of a widow—

veuve d'un époux vivant—

without a widow's freedom to remarry should she wish?

One would like to think that Abelard was concerned for Héloïse. And, so far as was consistent with his egoism, he probably was concerned. Moreover, the fact that his mother had taken the veil, when her husband had entered a monastery, would make it appear the more natural that Héloïse should do so. There is a further point. Writing later to Héloïse he uses, in referring to the marriage, the words: "When I wanted to keep for myself for all time you whom I loved beyond measure." [*cum cuperem te mihi supra modum dilectam in perpetuum retinere.*] A person's capacity for love and the manner in which love finds expression is related to the character as a whole. The selfish person loves selfishly; the unselfish person unselfishly; the courageous person with courage; the timid with timidity. Abelard liked to dominate and possess. And so he loved possessively, jealously. He had married Héloïse, he says, to keep her for himself, for ever. He was determined still to keep her. Here, in changed circumstances, was a way of doing so. Inside the convent walls, her life dedicated to the service of God, she would belong to no human being—to none other than Abelard. And that is not all. In the knowledge that Héloïse was in a convent not only was he secure from rivals, he was saved from being alone in his adversity. She whom he was afterwards to call his "inseparable companion", must suffer with him.

In the *Historia Calamitatum* Abelard is telling his own story. He writes of Héloïse only in so far as she comes into this. Having described, therefore, with a vividness and a dramatic touch that suggests that he was himself present, the occasion of her taking the veil, he leaves it at that. His only reference to her life as a nun at Argenteuil is a comment (in a letter years later) as to her excellence as prioress. There are those who suppose that certain twelfth-century memorial verses written at Argenteuil in honour of the Blessed Vital, founder of the abbey of Savigny, who died in 1121, are the work of Héloïse. If so, it is possible that the script in which they are written is also hers. The thought is an interesting one, but it carries no certainty. As to her personal life in the convent, nothing is known. That the harshness of her lot touched the imagination of her times is proved by the simple verses written by Walter Map, an Englishman who lived in the latter half of her century, in which he evokes the stunned

grief and the bewilderment of Héloïse during the period
immediately following her husband's withdrawal to Saint-
Denis:

> *Nupta querit ubi sit suus Palatinus,*
> *Cuius totus extitit spiritus divinus.*
> *Querit cur se substrahat quasi perigrinus,*
> *Quem ad sua ubera foverat et sinus.*

[The bride asks where is her Philosopher whose every word
was inspired. Why, she asks, does he withdraw, as if he were
a stranger—he whom she had enfolded in loving arms?]

CHAPTER IV

Ecce elongavi fugiens et mansi in solitudine.

[Lo, I have gone far off, fleeing away, and abode in the wilderness.]

Psalm 7,
Abelard. *Hist. Calam.* P.L. 159

THE abbey church of Saint-Denis is some six miles from the Ile de la Cité. The distance seemed to me greater than it is as I travelled north in the Métro, through station after station, through Pigalle and Marcadet to the Porte de la Chapelle. From there a bus crowded with workers wearing blue overalls rattled along a flat straight road past shabby dwelling-houses, shops, artisans' cafés, factories, warehouses. Somewhere to the right an iron bridge spanned the sluggish water of a canal. There was no grass and, apart from a few dusty planes, no trees. A gasometer occupied what in the Middle Ages had been the *Lendit* fair-ground.

Once the funeral processions of the kings of France had passed this way through open country, then along the twisting rue Boulangerie to the church that enshrined the tomb of the first bishop of Paris, Saint Dionysius or Denis who, the story runs, having been decapitated, along with the priest Rusticus and the deacon Eleutherius, on what is now the hill of Montmartre, walked to the place of his burial, carrying his head in his hand. Another account, which disposes of the necessity of the saint having to carry his head, puts the site of his death in the district that was known in ancient times as Vicus Catholicus and is now occupied by the abbey and the neighbouring streets.

This royal abbey where the kings of France before going
into battle received the *oriflamme* into their hands, where
many of them were crowned, and, along with their queens
and their children, many buried, has a history at once glorious
and terrible. In the Middle Ages it was the seed-ground of
councillors, statesmen, scholars, saints. Men used to speak
not of "Saint-Denis near Paris", but "Paris near Saint-Denis".
In Abelard's day, Louis VI called Saint-Denis the "head of
his kingdom". Seven hundred years later, after the Revolution
and the desecration of the royal tombs in 1793, Chateaubriand found a desert. Little children played among the bones
of kings, grass was growing on broken altars, rain dripped
through the gaping roof.

Today Saint-Denis has a rugged battered splendour—as of
a warrior scarred but undefeated. The once silver-pale stone
is blackened with soot and grime. The entrances under the
three round-arched porches might be the mouths of caverns
receding into darkness. The sturdy south tower, going back
to the twelfth century, stands up, with none to match it on
the north side, solitary and triumphant. The church looks its
most imposing not in sunlight, but under a leaden sky that
threatens thunder, or under a sky heavy with snow. Utrillo,
when he painted Saint-Denis in winter, gave as much attention to the sky as to the abbey. And to anyone who, unable to
travel to Paris, would yet like to know something of Saint-
Denis, I would say: "Look at Utrillo's painting. And when
you have meditated on this and allowed it to speak to you
and to tell you, as it surely will, something about the spirit
of the abbey—then, but not before, look at photographs and
read books."

Once commanding an extensive view of the fertile, smiling
countryside of the Ile de France, the abbey is now cluttered
about. Small ancient streets proper to the scene are losing
their identity before the inroads of industrialisation. Yet the

abbey transcends a setting that is unworthy of itself. It has known too much change for change to spoil it. It stands unperturbed, dignified, a little aloof, looking across the marketplace towards the grim rather pretentious Hôtel de Ville.

When Abelard became a monk at Saint-Denis in the year 1119, the abbey was in the main the comparatively small and simple basilica that had been built in the seven hundreds under the direction of Abbot Fulrad on the site of Dagobert's earlier church. In it Pépin-le-Bref was crowned; and when he came to die he asked, for humility's sake, that he might be buried under the porch where pilgrims would trample over his grave. To Fulrad's church, of which there are traces in the crypt, there was added in the ninth century the chapel of Hilduin. Its fat sturdy pillars, each like a giant altarcandle, still stand, enclosed within Abbot Suger's twelfth-century crypt.

Abbot Suger was born in 1081 (two years after Abelard) of humble parentage, probably at Argenteuil. He was educated at the abbey school of Saint-Denis, where he was in the company of the young Prince Louis (afterwards Louis VI) with whom he formed a life-long friendship. A small man of weak stature but vast drive and determination, he played a long and vigorous role at court. Having become a monk at Saint-Denis, he was councillor to Louis VI and tutor to his son. When the latter succeeded to the throne, Suger accompanied him to Bordeaux for the marriage of the young king to Catherine of Aquitaine. From then on Suger appeared less in public. Withdrawing to Saint-Denis where he had become abbot in 1123 (roughly two years after Abelard took his vows) he devoted himself to what had been his ambition since boyhood—the reconstruction and ornamentation of the abbey. Abelard and Bernard of Clairvaux expressed themselves through the spoken and the written word, Suger through the medium of stone and glass. It was under his direction that

the Romanesque gave place to the Gothic at Saint-Denis, as
it did later in the century in Paris. His windows, restored
and depleted though they now are, shine in a jewelled radiance of emerald and azure, crimson and gold, upon the abbey's darkness. The imagination soars, as was his intention,
to a luminous, transcendental world of saints and angels, and
then drops again to earth as the eye is caught by the plump,
prosaic figure of a monk prostrate (in the window of the
Annunciation) before the Virgin—and, in the glass above
him, are the words: *Sugerius Abbas*.

Abelard did not find at Saint-Denis the peace for which he
had hoped. The monks, he says, were unruly and dissolute;
the abbot (this was Adam, the predecessor of Suger) no better than the rest. There is no reason to think that he exag-
gerates—what he says is borne out by records of the abbey,
as well as by Saint Bernard whose criticisms precipitated the
reforms subsequently introduced by Suger. However, Abelard
did not make matters easier for himself. One might have
supposed that, in view of his own unhappy circumstances, he
would have kept in the background. Had he done so he would
not have been Abelard. On the contrary, he felt it incumbent
upon him to reform his brethren. With a naïveté—or was it
obtuseness?—past belief, he took them to task continually in
private and in public, reproaching them for their evil ways.
Not surprisingly they resented this, so that soon he had become in their eyes "detestable beyond measure". At length
he was permitted to remove himself to a priory at Maison-
celle, near Provins in the district of Champagne, where he
began to teach again. But while, as formerly, he delighted his
students, he made enemies among his contemporaries by his
arrogance. Enmity probably played its part in bringing about
the condemnation at the council of Soissons in 1121 of his
recently published work: *De unitate et trinitate divina*. Accused of having tried to divide the indivisible Godhead he

was ordered—despite his assurances that nothing was further from his intention—to throw his book into the flames. "They compelled me to throw my book with my own hands into the fire, and it was burnt up": *et sic combustus est*.

In so real a sense is a book part of the writer; so intimately is its destiny linked with his own, that Abelard's distress is not to be wondered at. Anguish and bitterness welled up within him. In a frenzy of grief that was hardly short of despair he could only call upon his Saviour, expostulating with him in the words of Saint Antony the Hermit: *Jesu bone, ubi es?* [Good Jesus, where art Thou?] The maiming of his body —that he could accept as being what he had deserved. His book was another matter. He had written it in a spirit of devotion to his faith; in an attempt to make this same faith intelligible to reason, to present it in a manner that would help those who had complained that "the utterance of words not comprehended by the intellect is useless". Moreover, as a further penalty he was committed to custody at the abbey of Saint-Medard, a monastery to which, it was said, the unlettered used to be sent for instruction, the licentious to be corrected, the perverse to be subdued. This, as well as being an insult, was a farce. The abbot and the monks realised it, and they did what they could to console him. Soon, since there was widespread indignation at his treatment, he was released and sent back to Saint-Denis. Here trouble was again in store for him, and again it was of his own making. Already in disfavour with his brethren for his persistent criticism of their misdeeds, he now found it necessary to put them right on the subject of the abbey's patron saint. Dionysius or Denis, the bishop of Paris, Abelard had discovered—and he could not resist making public his discovery—was not the same person as Dionysius the Areopagite, as had hitherto been believed, but quite another. Once again Abelard had

unleashed against himself a tempest of fury. And the more
he argued, the greater was the fury.

When Suger became abbot of Saint-Denis Abelard's position improved. Dispensed from living in the monastery, he
withdrew once more to Champagne, to a lonely stretch of
country, *ad solitudinem quandam,* by the river Arduzon, near
Nogent-sur-Seine, in the direction of Troyes. There, having
received a gift of land, he built with the consent of the bishop
an oratory made of reeds and thatch, in honour of the Holy
Trinity. At first he was alone but for one cleric. This, however, was not for long. His former students came flocking to
him: "they came hurrying from every direction, leaving cities
and towns to be with me in my solitude. Instead of spacious
homes they built themselves huts; instead of tasty food they
lived on herbs and coarse bread; instead of soft beds they slept
on mattresses of thatch and straw; instead of tables they used
piled turf." They provided Abelard with food and clothing
and, since the oratory was too small for so many, they rebuilt
it of stone and wood. His students held him in the highest
esteem. To them he was the philosopher of all philosophers.
His wit and his quick mind delighted them; he was the *rhinoceros indomitus* ("the rhinoceros that could not be tamed")
who tossed his opponents on the horn of his dialectical brilliance. One of his students, an Englishman named Hilary,
has left verses in which he seeks to appease the master who,
angered at a rumour brought to him by a servant, has threat-
ened to turn away his pupils and make them live at the nearby
village of Quincey. The poem is in part an attack on the tell-
tale servant, in part a plea to the master to have pity on his
devotees:

> Desolatos, magister, respice
> Spemque nostram, quae languet, refice,

[Look upon us, master, in our desolation and revive our wilting hope.]

When the oratory was rebuilt, Abelard had it dedicated afresh—this time to the Paraclete, the Holy Spirit, the Comforter who had brought him solace in his adversities. This gesture, harmless though it may seem, involved him in yet more trouble. His enemies, jealous at his following of students, found fault, saying that it was contrary to tradition, if not unlawful, to dedicate a church to the Holy Spirit. Like his accusers at Soissons, they were suggesting that, in singling out one Person of the Trinity, he was by implication dividing the indivisible Godhead—a charge which, as he relates the incident in the *Historia Calamitatum*, he vehemently refutes. His peace was destroyed. Rumours about him spread, "like Echo in the poet's fable". He came to dread any gathering of clerics, imagining that they had met to accuse him of heresy. So unnerved did he become that he contemplated withdrawing from Christendom, believing that he was more likely to find peace among the heathen.

In the midst of these afflictions, when he was more than ever disposed to take himself off in the hope of finding Christ among the enemies of Christ, he fell into the company of monks yet more uncouth, more base than were those of Saint-Denis. For it came about that he was invited, probably in the year 1126, to become abbot of Saint-Gildas-de-Rhuys, in the diocese of Vannes in Brittany.

"Never, God knows, would I have agreed to this suggestion had I not been determined, as I have said, to escape somehow or other from these endless persecutions." The words are Abelard's and I was reading them by the flickering light from a cluster of white-stemmed votive candles as I sat in the great sombre granite cathedral in Vannes, wondering if the rain would ever stop. I had arrived from Paris on an August day so cold that it might have been January. A north-east wind was blowing the rain before it, sheet after sheet of it. I had been aware only of the rain. I had not yet seen Vannes, the real Vannes: the mediaeval ramparts, towers and archways; cobbled streets twisting and climbing between ancient bulging houses; gardens ablaze with flowers; a harbour sprigged with the sails of yachts; restaurants that specialise in rare seafoods.

And yet the bad weather had served a purpose in that it had awakened in me a compassion for Abelard that I had not known before: a sudden realisation of his loneliness and despair. I pushed open the heavy door of the cathedral. The rain was still pouring down, making rivulets among the cobbles, leaping up in little spouts. I made a dash into a café. It was a long narrow room: a couple of candles were burning, and at the far end workmen with swarthy faces were talking together in low intense voices. I sat down at a wooden table on which there was a carafe of wine. A plump, smiling girl came over to me, carrying an immense bowl of soup which she began ladling out. A white and black cat with a flat head and short thick fur appeared out of the shadows, then, giving a silent spring, settled on a chair facing me. He sat up very straight, his eyes like yellow moons.

The abbey of Saint-Gildas-de-Rhuys is about twenty miles from Vannes, on a granite headland overlooking on one side the Gulf of Morbihan, on the other the Atlantic. It stands back from a village of the same name, built on what was once the Roman road running between Vannes and Port-Navallo. It was a charming village, I thought, when I came to it in the morning sunshine. Its winding street took me with disconcerting suddenness to an open space (there was a fig-tree there, I remember, and round its trunk a wooden seat) in front of an austere Romanesque church of which the apse and ambulatory go back to the eleventh century. "Abelard would have seen these," M. le Curé murmured as he glanced up at the neat, rounded arches that remain in my mind not so much as I saw them then as on a later occasion when they were caught in the light of the setting sun. They glowed, that evening, a warm bronze-red that carried my thoughts back to the Mesquita del Cristo de la Luz in Toledo—a shadowy bronze-red church, formerly a mosque then dedicated to Christ the Light of the World, crowded with little horse-shoe arches repeating one another like an echo heard in the dusk.

Saint Gildas was born in the year 494. According to a record in the library at Vannes, he was a native of Bath and a pupil of Saint Iltud. He came to Brittany, the Curé told me, from Scotland, and lived for some time in solitude on the Ile de Houat, in the gulf of Morbihan. The land on which he eventually built a church and monastery was given to him by a *seigneur* called Guereche who had a château on the site of a Roman camp that guarded the road. In his old age Saint Gildas withdrew to his island where he died in the year 565. His body, which was found in a boat floating in the gulf, was brought to the church where it was buried behind the high altar. A century after his death the monastery had a reputation for learning—in particular for the study of theology and the Scriptures. By the eleven hundreds this was a thing of the past. A parochial history records that at this time the doors of the church were decorated with the paws of deer, and that the monks' day began not with prayer but with the sounding of the hunting-horn and the braying of hounds. But that was not the worst. Abelard's spiritual sons proved to be no better than brigands and assassins. Moreover, as abbot he found himself expected to provide them with the wherewithal to keep their concubines and children.

Beyond the church, and entered through what is now the convent of Les Sœurs de la Charité de Saint-Louis, are monastic buildings going back to the thirteenth century. On three sides (the south wall of the church forms the fourth) cloisters with rounded arches and, above these, shuttered windows, enclose a pleasantly informal garden that was bright with marigolds, petunias, pansies, and the first dahlias. The warm air was laden with the scents of flowers. An insect hummed. A nun carrying a tray weighed down with crockery smiled at me as she passed. The community was founded, after the Revolution, for the care of Breton children, by Madame Molé de Champlatreux after her young husband (whom she loved deeply, as he did her) had been guillotined. Different though her life was from that of Héloïse, she resembled the latter in intelligence, courage, and warmth of heart.

On the far side of the cloisters a field-track took me down to the cliff-edge. Gorse was in flower and sea-holly. To the left, past a stone wall enclosing the garden of the abbey, there was a well surmounted by a cross wreathed in honeysuckle; and, again to the left, a dark copse of ilex-trees, their branches contorted by the wind. A salt tang hung upon the air and gulls mewed. A brilliantly blue sea shadowed with amethyst and jade and crinkled by each passing wind reached away to meet the paler, silky, blue of the sky. One could not have wished for a more tranquil scene. But there are other days at Saint-Gildas-de-Rhuys, when the wind howls; when the waves batter the rocks, thudding and hissing, tossing the spray as they swish and roar, tunnelling their way into the cliffs. Abelard had disliked the sound of the sea—he mentions the harsh, roaring waves: *horrisoni undas oceani*. He was utterly alone, cut off from congenial companionship and from all intellectual stimuli—a stranger and an exile. The dialect spoken at Saint-Gildas was unintelligible to him. The fact that he was himself a Breton did not help. For Le Pallet, his birthplace, is on the extreme edge of Brittany, almost in Touraine. Besides, he had spent practically his entire manhood out of Brittany. Though proud of his origins he thought of himself as belonging to France (the two regions were still separate, Brittany being under the rule of a duke) which he mentions in a letter to Héloïse as being his country and hers. In his distress he made his own the words of the psalmist: *A finibus terrae ad te clamavi dum anxiaretur cor meum.* [To thee have I cried from the ends of the earth when my heart was in anguish.] The uselessness of his life weighed upon him. Here he was achieving nothing. And he had abandoned the oratory of the Paraclete and, with it, his students. He saw himself as a failure: a man who could bring nothing to completion.

Abelard's troubles were at their height when he received news that the convent at Argenteuil, where Héloïse was now prioress, had been taken over by Suger, abbot of Saint-Denis, who claimed to have documentary evidence that the convent had been the property of the abbey since the reign of Pépin: Suger also brought an accusation that some of the community were leading irregular lives. It is difficult, if not impossible, at this distance of time to assess with certainty the rights and wrongs of the case. But whether technically Suger had right on his side, his behaviour was high-handed. Without waiting for the nuns to find another home, he "flung them out": *violenter expelleret.*[9] In telling of this Abelard mentions Héloïse for the first time since describing the occasion of her taking the veil at Argenteuil nearly ten years before Suger's action. Did Héloïse and Abelard meet during those years? Did Abelard visit Argenteuil? Were letters exchanged? There is no evidence one way or another. All we know is that now, hearing what Suger had done, Abelard acted immediately.

Having travelled from Saint-Gildas-de-Rhuys to the Paraclete on the far side of Paris (a distance in all of some three hundred and sixty miles) and having forthwith obtained permission of Hatto, bishop of Troyes, he arranged that the oratory and the land about it should be made over to Héloïse and those of her nuns who wished to remain with her. This was in 1129. By January 30th, 1131, Abelard had not returned to Brittany, for it was on that date that he met Pope Innocent II near Etampes (Bernard of Clairvaux was present), as a result of which the foundation of the convent of the Paraclete was confirmed in a papal bull in which Héloïse was described as prioress of the Oracle of the Holy Trinity. She was, however, subsequent to this, until her death, acknowledged in papal bulls and other documents as abbess of the Paraclete. As such she did more, Abelard says, in one year than he could have done in a hundred. Such grace, he says, did the Lord bestow upon her that "bishops loved her as a daughter, abbots as a sister, the laity as a mother, while all without exception marvelled at her goodness, her wisdom, and, on every occasion, her extraordinary gentleness and patience". He adds that she seldom appeared in public, but that this meant she was the more sought after.

After making over the Paraclete to Héloïse, Abelard at first kept aloof from the convent, wanting to avoid criticism. As a result he was reproached for neglecting the new foundation. He then made frequent visits, preaching and giving such advice and help as he could. But this again brought him reproaches. So he could not bear, his enemies taunted, to be parted from the woman whom he had loved when in the world. The fact is (we have his word for this) that had he been free to follow his inclination he would have chosen to pass the remainder of his days at the Paraclete, that "haven of peace away from the tempest and tumult". But this was not to be. Like Cain, he says, he was destined to be a wanderer and a fugitive, harried from place to place. Angry voices were raised against him. What was he doing, the abbot of

Saint-Gildas, away from his sons to whom duty, if nothing else, bound him? And so he returned to his monastery.

At Saint-Gildas his monks made attempts to kill him. They put poison in his food and drink and, when this failed, in his chalice at Mass. The mention of the chalice is evidence that by this time Abelard had been ordained a priest. Another attempt to poison him (on this occasion through the agency of a servant) was made when he was away from the abbey, staying in the house of his brother in Nantes. Moreover, he narrowly escaped death at the hands of brigands posted on the roadside for this purpose. He also had a fall from his horse, fracturing a bone in his neck; the accident caused him intense and prolonged pain, worse than that resulting from the mutilation. Eventually, on the authority of the papal legate, he compelled some of the monks to leave Saint-Gildas. This, however, availed little, since those who remained proved yet worse; an attempt was even made to put a dagger through his throat. He compares his plight to that of Damocles over whose head there hung, ever ready to fall, a sword suspended by a thread.

CHAPTER V

IT appears that Abelard wrote the *Historia Calamitatum* at the abbey of Saint-Gildas; for, towards the end, he mentions the dangers to which at the time of writing he was still exposed: *in quo etiam adhuc laboro periculo*. He must have completed it between the years 1131 and 1136, since he refers to the brief of Innocent II, dated November 28th, 1131, confirming the cession of the Paraclete to Héloïse; and in 1136 he was back in Paris, teaching on Mont Sainte-Geneviève where John of Salisbury, friend of Thomas à Becket, was among his pupils. He does not tell us his motive in writing. Possibly it was a desire to assess his past and justify it. Or he may have hoped, by drawing attention to former triumphs, to prepare the way for a return to the arena of dialectic.

It has become a commonplace to say that the Middle Ages, familiar to us though certain aspects of them are, in other respects are more remote from our own age than is classical Greece. The mediaeval world has given us, in its churches, the perfection of the Romanesque followed by the flowering of the Gothic: the figures on the west front of Chartres and Suger's glass glowing in the darkness of Saint-Denis. It has given us the weight and the erudition of Saint Thomas Aquinas and, at the other end of the scale, the scholars' lyrics, delicate in their beauty, carrying upon them the breath of the wind, the scent of flowers, the heart's pain and its joy. Yet this period, if set against that of fifth-century Athens, is, at least at first sight, inarticulate. There are philosophers in plenty, but not one who can do what Plato does, which is to bring to life through the sheer grace of his writing an entire world, so that in reading him we do more than listen to a disquisition on justice, truth, or the immortality of the soul— we encounter human beings with idiosyncrasies like our own; we hear the wind stirring in a plane-tree, the tinkling of a stream, the scolding of the cicadas in the season of the dog-star. Nor in the Middle Ages are there the giants of tragic drama: there is no Aeschylus nor Sophocles nor Euripides to speak to the heart through characters whose anguish is a reflection of that of all mankind. And yet, despite this being so, it is in its response to human sensibilities that the twelfth century of the Christian era has a quality which sets it apart from the centuries immediately before and after. The rediscovery of the classical past meant that an increasing number of educated persons not merely drew on Seneca, Juvenal, Persius, Lucan, Virgil, Horace, and Ovid (the Greeks were as yet known mostly in translations into Latin) to adorn the spoken and the written word—they were able to express themselves in an easy, fluent Latin which they used as a medium to relate their day-to-day experiences, reveal their likes and dislikes, attitudes and emotions. The letters of Bernard of Clairvaux, the letters of Peter the Venerable, the life story of Ailred of Rievaulx, Suger's account of his work at Saint-Denis—all these have in common a directness and naturalness of expression which bridges the gulf between ourselves and the writers.

These men are not remote figures of history: we feel that we
know what kind of persons they were. And still more is this
true of Héloïse and Abelard. To read the correspondence[10]
that passed between them is not only to become the spectator
of a drama, it is to overhear an exchange between two persons which seems now to be intended for all the world to
hear, now to be meant for these two alone; one in which,
sometimes deliberately, sometimes with no such intent, the
innermost conflicts of heart, mind, and will are laid bare. At
times the language assumes, as was the fashion of the day, the
studied artificiality of rhetoric—weighed down as it is with
appeals to authorities from the Christian and the classical
past. More often it is direct, sometimes to the point of blunt
realism. From time to time it becomes lyrical; this is true
particularly of the writing of Héloïse whose Latin, perhaps
because she was less inhibited, less self-conscious than Abelard, is more flowing, more musical. It is unlikely that either
had read Catullus (his manuscripts were few at this period),
but in precision of thought, boldness of expression, intensity
of emotion, and lyricism, the letters recall the Roman poet
who immortalised the ecstasy and the torment of love.

The *Historia Calamitatum*, though included as part of the
correspondence, is not addressed to Héloïse. It purports to
be a letter written by Abelard to a friend (possibly a fellow-
scholar) in distress. The writer, however, engrossed in his own
misfortunes, proceeds, after the opening, to ignore the friend,
reverting to him (and then in a somewhat cavalier fashion)
only towards the end. There is, indeed, no evidence that any
such friend existed: the fact that Héloïse (when writing to
Abelard) appears to believe in his existence proves nothing,
since she may have decided to play the role of believing what
Abelard apparently wished her to believe. The epistolary form
was an accepted literary device, a framework in which to set

the narrative, borrowed from Cicero or Plato, who often give their views in a dialogue between friends.

Apart from its content the interest of the *Historia Calamitatum* lies in the fact that, having come into the hands of Héloïse, it elicited from her the first of her letters to Abelard (the first, that is to say, that is extant, for it is not impossible that there were others), thus enabling posterity to hear her speak in her own voice. It is true that Abelard in telling his story records the arguments that she used in trying to dissuade him from the marriage and that Héloïse confirms these as being, as far as they go, correct. But, apart from one sentence, they are presented in his words, not hers.

A reader coming to the *Historia Calamitatum* for the first time may well be offended by the vast egoism of the author. What kind of man is this who, throughout a lengthy discourse on his intellectual career, has not a word of appreciation for those who taught him; who sees no philosopher other than himself as deserving of recognition; who makes no mention of his fellow-scholars unless it be to enhance his own fame? No less insufferable is his tone in relating the story of himself and Héloïse—the emphasis on his intellectual brilliance, his fame, his good looks, his condescension in loving her; his cleverness in deceiving Fulbert. But what Abelard has written must be seen against its background. Bombast such as his is a cover for a sense of inadequacy. A man reasonably satisfied with his attainments feels no need to exaggerate his value. But even in his youth Abelard, despite his gifts, had doubted his worth. Hence his disparagement of his masters, his persistent and exaggerated efforts to prove himself superior to others. The illness which took him back to Brittany is significant. It points not to overwork (to which he attributes it), but to tension conditioned by strife and rivalry. And much had happened between then and the writing of the *Historia Calamitatum*. There had been the mutilation. In his account of this, one emotion clouds all others, and that is shame: a fear of public humiliation: the thought that henceforth he will appear ridiculous in men's eyes is the supreme torment. Then a further shame awaited him in his condemnation at Soissons and the burning, by his own hands, of his book. Moreover, he could adjust himself to circumstances neither at Saint-Denis nor at Saint-Gildas (whether this was his fault or not is irrelevant); and when he made over the Paraclete to Héloïse, this exposed him to obloquy, first for neglecting his foundation, then for paying it too much attention. Returning to Brittany he was met with persistent threats to his life. As Abelard looks back over the years he sees behind him a trail of disappointment and failure. At his wits' end, he tries pathetically, by exaggerating his own triumphs and depreciating those of others, to repair the shattered image of his self-esteem. We may not like what we hear, but the voice that speaks is authentic. If it provokes our indignation, it also invites our compassion.

Héloïse writing to Abelard after she has read the *Historia Calamitatum* says that it has recently come into her possession *by chance*. It may have seemed chance to her. Or there may have been irony in her words. For, if chance brought Abelard's letter to Héloïse, it was surely a chance that he had himself contrived. Then going on to speak of the content, she uses the word *memini* [I remember] which suggests that the manuscript was no longer with her. Being in the nature of an autobiographical essay rather than a private communication, it may have been passed from one to another of Abelard's friends and relatives. In any case, Héloïse has no need of the manuscript: the story it tells is already graven on her memory, so violent has been its impact.

When she had seen at a glance that the handwriting was Abelard's she began to read eagerly, thinking to find comfort in the words of him whom she loved no less now than formerly. Her hopes were dashed. In almost every line she found, she says, gall and wormwood: *verba fere omnia felle et absintho plena.* Bitter indeed was first the record of his misfortunes (some of them already familiar, others new to her) culminating in the dangers that still at the time of completing the *Historia Calamitatum* were threatening his life. Woven into this was the personal story of Abelard and herself, told in a manner that could not fail to be hurtful to one who had loved him with a disinterested selfless love, the reality of which she had proved by her actions and was continuing to prove up to the present moment. What were her thoughts as she read his narrative, boastful and self-centred as it was, of the calculated seduction of a young girl by her tutor? There was little that told of love in this—or in his smug satisfaction at having deceived his host; or in the complacent assumption that, with so much to commend him, he had no cause to fear a rebuff.

He had, it is true, acknowledged certain of her qualities— her looks, her intellectual gifts, her good sense and foresight. But all this he had told in relation to himself, stressing on the one hand his cleverness in having chosen to love a woman superior to others of her sex; on the other, his misfortune in having suffered as a result (as he saw it) of this love. He had shown no appreciation of the magnitude of the sacrifice that Héloïse had made for him in becoming a nun; no regret for the suffering that he on his part had brought upon her; no regret for having been the cause of alienating her from her uncle; or for having separated her from her child, the anticipation of whose birth had filled her with joy.

Reading on she had been met with the words: "Héloïse now my sister in Christ rather than my wife": *iam in Christo soror potius quam uxor Heloisa.* Abelard was making clear to his reader—any reader into whose hands his manuscript might

come—that the abbess of the Paraclete was the same Héloïse
whose story he had left suspended at the point when she took
her vows at Argenteuil. He was not denying that she was his
wife. He could not do that: not even their joint entry into
religion could efface the seal set upon each by the sacrament
of marriage. They were husband and wife, even though outwardly they no longer lived as such. But Abelard's words were
ill-chosen. He was intellectually brilliant, but he did not understand human nature. At every step in his career—as a
young student, a lecturer, a monk at Saint-Denis, as abbot of
Saint-Gildas—he had alienated others by his high-handedness
and lack of tact. And now Héloïse is distressed not by what
he says, but the way in which he says it: the fact that the
words emphasise the gulf separating him from her, rather
than the inner bond that continued and must always continue
to unite them. At a distance of eight hundred years his words
strike chill. How then did they seem to Héloïse? What could
they have seemed but a denial or, if not a denial, a rejection
of the past? And to some extent this is what they were. Abelard was a monk now. All that had occurred in the rue des
Chantres; all that had led up to the marriage; the attempt to
conceal the marriage; Fulbert's vengeance; the motives gov-
erning his own decision to withdraw to Saint-Denis; his insistence that Héloïse should not only become a religious, but do
so before he had himself taken his vows—to be reminded was
to be confronted with guilt and shame. In telling his story
in the *Historia Calamitatum* he had put the past behind him.

   Soror potius quam uxor. [Sister rather than wife.] The
words rankle in the mind of Héloïse. She reflects on their
significance (and by implication would have Abelard do the
same) in the superscription that heads her reply; in what is
a masterpiece of understatement and irony, as compressed as
an epigram by a writer of classical Rome; one in which, as in
a poem, the heart speaks but emotions are distilled. Whom,

she asks, is she addressing? What is the relationship of Abelard to herself, herself to Abelard? In the old days she had called him her master—Abelard, the master of the Paris schools, the master who had taught her logic and the humanities in her uncle's house in the rue des Chantres—the master, too, of her heart. But is it not more fitting to call the founder of the religious house of which she is the abbess, her father; and herself not his handmaid, as once, but his daughter? Abelard is her husband. Yet he has chosen to call her his sister, in which case he is her brother; and if he is her brother, then she is no longer his wife, but as he has himself written, his sister. Thus taking possible titles of address, she sets one against another, discards the one she prefers in favour of what, she must presume, is Abelard's choice. Master gives place to father, husband to brother; handmaid to daughter, wife to sister. And yet, by whatever title each may address the other, they are as from the beginning and will always be Abelard and Héloïse. *Domino suo imo patri, coniugi suo imo fratri, ancilla sua imo filia, ipsius uxor imo soror, Abelardo Heloisa.* [To her master or rather father, to her husband or rather brother; his handmaid or rather daughter, his wife or rather sister; to Abelard, Héloïse.]

The letter that follows is a plea that Abelard should write to her. She wants passionately to hear from him. Her warm nature cries out for an acknowledgement that, though time, distance, circumstances, separate them, the inner bond uniting one to the other is unbroken. Abelard may wish to forget that she is his wife, but Héloïse has no wish to forget it. He had insisted upon marriage and she had argued against it for his sake. Now it is she who wants a recognition (in the only way possible) of their relationship. She has another reason for wanting a letter from him—that her anxiety on his account (an anxiety that results partly from a long silence, partly from

what she has read of the dangers to which he is exposed),
may at least in part be allayed. As it is she waits at the Paraclete in dread that each day will bring news of his death. She
would have him tell her all, that in return she may give him
the sympathy he needs and that her heart aches to give. In
times of distress, she reminds him, sympathy brings solace.
The community at the Paraclete is eager to carry with him
a burden that in being shared will be the lighter. Now and
later Héloïse makes a point of mentioning her nuns, to give
Abelard a further reason, seeing that the Paraclete is his, to
share his news, bad or good, with those who are in very truth
his friends. For whatever his news, she would have him write,
if it be only to show that he is not forgetful of those who
have him ever in mind. True to her century she appeals to the
authority of Seneca who, in writing to Lucilius, thanks him
because by means of a letter he has brought, as it were face
to face, friends who otherwise would have been apart. This,
she says, is something that Abelard, no less than Lucilius, can
do. There is nothing to stop him unless it be his own negligence. He owes this to his daughters in Christ. The Paraclete
is the vineyard that he himself has planted. As such it stands
in need of his care.

Héloïse sees the Paraclete, the religious house of which
Abelard is the founder and herself the abbess, as the bond
that will unite them. Taking up his complaint in the *Historia
Calamitatum* that he was achieving nothing in his abbey in
Brittany, she asks him with some vigour why, then, does he
waste his efforts? The monks at Saint-Gildas will not listen
to him—his eloquence and his learning are in vain—whereas
at the Paraclete she and her nuns need him and wait for him.
If he will pay to his daughters in Christ the debt that as their
founder he owes to them, he will at the same time be paying
the far greater debt he owes to her who is especially—indeed,
in a unique manner—his own.

Héloïse does more than ask Abelard to allay her anxiety.
She is doing more than offering sympathy. At a time when, as
his own words have made clear, he is not only in danger of his
life but so harried on every side, so discouraged in his every
enterprise (he has been a failure at Saint-Denis and Saint-
Gildas, condemned as a heretic at Soissons, and his book con-
signed to the flames) that he has scarcely any longer the will
to live or the power to project his thoughts beyond the con-
fines of his own miseries—at this time she gives him, by stressing his obligation to the convent of the Paraclete and more
especially to herself, an incentive to rouse himself out of a
lethargy that verges upon despair. She had read his summing
up of his predicament—that he was as one who having begun
to build could not finish. Here at the Paraclete, she tells him,
a task awaits him.

The prevailing tone of the letter is one of tender solicitude.
But it is spirited and challenging; indignant and then again
ironic. How is it, she asks, that, having before him the example of the Fathers of the Church who from earliest times
wrote treatises for the help and encouragement and the comfort of women, he has done nothing of the kind for her?
Though she became a religious at his bidding she has received
no word of comfort either from him in person (that is, when
he was at the Paraclete at the time of establishing the convent) or by letter. Is not this the more strange seeing that she
is united to him not only by the marriage sacrament, *nuptialis
foedere sacramenti*, but also by a love to which she has set no
limits; *immoderato amore*. He knows very well, and so does
everyone else ("You know my beloved and everyone knows":
Nosti, charissime, noverunt omnes) the unhappiness that is
hers in consequence of being parted from her husband. It
rests, then, with him to give her comfort: "You alone can
make me sad, make me joyful or comfort me"; *Solus quippe es
qui contristare, qui me laetificare, seu consolari valeas.* He

knows that she fulfilled his every wish. In consenting to enter religion she had gone to the length of destroying her very self; she had allowed her love of him to reach such a pitch of madness that she robbed herself irreparably of the one thing she desired above all else, to share her life with his. She is telling him (for either he has never fully realised the truth or else he has forgotten) that she put on the habit of a nun, concealed her human feelings beneath the exterior proper to a nun, from one motive only, to prove that body and soul she was his. The taking of the vows at Argenteuil was the consummation of all that had gone before: "Nothing (God be my witness) have I ever sought in you other than yourself. You alone and not what was yours have I desired": *Nihil unquam (Deus scit) in te nisi te requisivi; te pure, non tua concupiscens.*

These words of Héloïse bring her to the marriage. A wife, as compared with a mistress, has the blessing of the Church, and in addition security: *nomen uxoris sacrius et validius.* Even so, she had thought it preferable to be Abelard's mistress or (if he will pardon her plain-speaking) his concubine or whore, because (her reasons are stated with precision) she believed that the more she humbled herself for his sake, the more favour would she win in his eyes and the less would she detract from the glory of his reputation. One has only to recall the arguments that, according to Abelard's account, she used in trying to dissuade him from the marriage. The *Historia Calamitatum* fresh in her mind, Héloïse confirms that she did use these arguments. But, she goes on, Abelard had passed over some of them, omitting to say that she had preferred love to marriage, freedom to a bond: *amorem coniugio, libertatem vinculo.* And now at the time of writing—when she is no longer the young girl who argued with her lover in Brittany but the abbess of the Paraclete—she thinks no differently. Given the circumstances she would say the same

again. Though the world be laid at her feet, she would choose
humiliation if it be for Abelard's good. Yes, had the emperor
Augustus deigned to honour her with marriage, made the
entire world over to her, still she would have chosen (it
would have been dearer to her and she would have thought
it more honourable) to be Abelard's mistress than to be wife
of the emperor of Rome: *carius mihi et dignius videretur tua
dici meretrix quam illius imperatrix.* Her use of the word
meretrix is deliberate. In the Middle Ages some indulgence
was conceded to concubinage, provided a permanent relationship was intended. *Meretrix* meant a prostitute, and Héloïse,
in choosing the word, pushes her argument to the furthest
extreme.

A seventeenth-century apologist of Héloïse, coming to her
defence against those who would twist her words into meaning that she advocated free love, says that she is speaking
figuratively in the manner of a poet, *figurate et poetice*—that
she is expressing in an outrush of devotion to her husband,
exuberantia conjugalis amoris, her contempt for worldly gain.
Her words, he goes on, are no more to be taken literally than
those put by Catullus into the mouth of his beloved when he
writes:

> *Nulli se dicit mulier mea nubere malle
> Quam mihi, non si Iuppiter ipse petat.*

[My beloved says that there is no one whom she would
rather marry than me, not even if Jupiter himself were to ask
her.]

Héloïse does not need an apologist. She has made herself
clear. She has not said that it is preferable to be a concubine
(still less a prostitute) than a wife. She has put the status of
wife on the plane to which it belongs. What she says is that
she deliberately chose the lower role (or would have done so

had Abelard agreed) rather than allow marriage to debar Abelard from reverting to a life consonant with the ideal of the celibate cleric-philosopher. To drive home this point she continues in her letter with a dissertation on the merits not of free love, but of marriage entered upon from true affection and not for material gain. In such a marriage a woman puts her husband before any advantage that could be hers. On the contrary, a woman who marries for what a man possesses and not for his own sake is selling herself, and consequently merits in return payment, not love.

As Héloïse writes, the past comes vividly before her. She is again the young girl in her uncle's home in the rue des Chantres, loved by the brilliant, versatile master of the cloister school. There had been no one like him. No king, no philosopher. When he appeared in public, people came hurrying to catch a glimpse of him. When he went away, they turned their heads to follow him with their gaze. She remembers the lyrics that he wrote and sang in her praise. Women envied her—the same who now feel compassion. And well they might feel compassion, for if, through consenting to the marriage, she caused Abelard's downfall, yet she was innocent in that in her intention there had been no evil. And it is not the deed but the intention that makes a crime; it is not what is done but the spirit in which it is done. As to her intention, Abelard knows the truth; he can pass judgement.

Héloïse loved passionately. But, for her, passion was only one aspect of love. Love worthy of the name must be disinterested. It must put the well-being of the beloved first. She was familiar either through the writings of Abelard and Saint Jerome or from having read Cicero (the *De Amicitia* was much read in her century) with the concept of *amicitia*. A general term indicating the disposition proper to a friend, it comprises kindness, tenderness, affection—all that goes to make a sincere and disinterested concern for another's welfare. Catullus in the early, happy days of his love had this concern for Lesbia:

> *Dilexi tum te non tantum ut vulgus amicam,*
> *Sed pater ut natos diligit et generos.*

[I loved you then not just as men commonly love a mistress, but as a father loves his sons and his sons-in-law.]

That Abelard should neglect to interest himself in the well-being of Héloïse; that he who is not only the founder of the Paraclete but her husband should take no steps to help her in the life that she is leading at his order, is in her eyes a grave defect. If in the first instance, she reminds him, he had felt for her true affection, his present neglect would be unthinkable. "Tell me one thing, if you can," she begins: *Dic unum, si vales.* She is on the point of asking him to tell her why it is that, after their having taken vows in religion—a course decided upon solely by him—he has not thought to give her a word of comfort, to write her a line of consolation. "Tell me, I say, if you can": *Dic, inquam, si vales.* But there is no need for him to do so. She already knows the answer: "It was lust not affection that bound you to me, the heat of passion not love". *Concupiscentia potius quam amicitia te mihi sociavit.* Yes, that is the answer. Now that he is deprived of the pleasures he once enjoyed, the tenderness he had shown only to win these pleasures has gone too. Indignation gives place to sadness as she reflects that this, indeed, is not her opinion alone. Others hold the same view. She would be happy were there someone to contradict her.

Concupiscentia potius quam amicitia. Abelard's account of his seduction of Héloïse is fresh in her mind. Hurt and indignant, she has taken this account, compressed it into a single sentence, confronted him with it. She is offering him a challenge. She is telling him that it is not too late: there is time still for him to show that, after all, he is not devoid of *amicitia*. The request she makes is a small one. If he cannot come to the Paraclete, he can write a letter. He can make this return for her having faced, as a young girl, the austerities of the religious life, and for having persevered in it to the present day.

It is from him alone that any reward can come to her. She can expect none from God (*nulla mihi . . . merces expectanda a Deo*), since she has done nothing for God. At the thought of her entry into the life of religion her indignation blazes afresh. She would willingly have followed Abelard as he "hastened" on his way to God. But that was not allowed her. Abelard had not trusted her. He had feared that, like Lot's wife, she would look back. How, she asks, could he have doubted her (the memory of this fills her with shame and fury) when at his bidding she had proved herself ready whether to follow, or precede, him into the very fires of hell: *ad Vulcania loca praecedere vel sequi?* It could not be otherwise. For her heart was not her own, but his. And it is still his. If it is not with him it is nowhere, for without him it does not exist: *Non enim mecum animus meus, sed tecum erat. Sed et nunc maxime si tecum non est, nusquam est. Esse vero sine te nequaquam potest.* Indignation gives place to tenderness as she makes a final appeal. In the past there had been those who had wondered whether she had loved Abelard or given in to him for a less worthy motive. The end has proved the beginning. For his sake she has denied herself all. She has kept nothing for herself but to be, now more than ever, his: *Nihil mihi reservavi, nisi sic tuam nunc praecipue fieri.* When he wanted her for his pleasure his letters had come in hot haste. And the name of Héloïse had been on the lips of all. All the squares and the homes of Paris rang with her name: *Me plateae omnes, me domus singulae resonabant.* Is it not

strange, then, that he does not show more zest in urging her
to the service of God?

In his reply to Héloïse, Abelard denies the charge of negligence. The fact that he had written her no word of comfort or
exhortation, he begs her to attribute not to neglect, but to her
wisdom in which he has the greatest confidence: *tuae de qua
semper plurinum confido prudentiae*. It is unnecessary, he
says, to address exhortations to one upon whom God's grace
has bestowed all that is needful. When she was prioress at
Argenteuil she had taught the erring, comforted the weak,
encouraged the faint-hearted. If, as he has every reason to
believe, as abbess of the Paraclete she cares for her daughters
with a like zeal, instruction on his part is superfluous. Yet, if
in her humility she thinks otherwise, she has only to tell him
and he will write, with God's help, on whatever subject she
has in mind. As for himself, he is in sore need of her prayers
and is sending a psalter for which [presumably when he was
at the Paraclete], she had earnestly begged him: *psalterium
quod a me sollicite requisisti*.

The tone of the letter is set in the superscription: *Heloisae
dilectissimae sorori suae in Christo Abelardus frater eius in
ipso*. [To Héloïse his most beloved sister in Christ, Abelard
her brother in the same.] And later it recurs when he addresses her: *soror in saeculo quondam chara, nunc in Christo
charissima*. [My sister once dear to me in the world, now most
dear in Christ.] They are words into which one can read much
or little, all or nothing. He is establishing, in fact, what he
considers to be the only relationship that, at any rate outwardly, is possible between them. But that does not mean
he denies or is indifferent to the deeper bond uniting them
to each other. It is hard to recognise, behind the guarded
words, the reckless Abelard of the days in the rue des Chantres. But even then there had been in his personality a vein

of secretiveness. On the one hand, he had blazoned abroad the name of Héloïse. On the other, he had tried to conceal the true nature of their relationship—under cover of his position as tutor; by sending her to Brittany in the disguise of a nun; by a secret marriage; by a denial that there had been a marriage; by putting her to live in the convent at Argenteuil. So now, having addressed her as his sister in Christ, he comes presently by a devious route to the point of acknowledging her as his wife. For having asked for the prayers of Héloïse and her nuns and enlarged—taking instances from the Scriptures—on the efficacy of the prayers of women, especially prayers offered by wives on behalf of husbands, he drops the plural "you", by which he had included the community in his address, and speaks to her alone whose goodness he is confident has power in the sight of God, and who, because he is specially hers, is in duty bound to help him in his tribulations—making it clear that it is precisely because she is his wife that she is thus empowered.

A warmth hitherto lacking has come into his words: "Listen, I beg you, with the ear of the heart to what you have heard many times with the ear of the body." *Exaudi, obsecro, aure cordis, quod saepius audisti aure corporis.* "A virtuous woman is a crown to her husband"—this is his theme. Verse after verse from the Scriptures is quoted: "Whosoever findeth a wife findeth a good thing and obtains a favour of the Lord." "Houses and riches are the inheritance of fathers. A prudent wife is from the Lord." "Blessed is the man that hath a virtuous wife." "A good wife is a good portion." He passes from the Old Testament to the New: "The unbelieving husband is sanctified by the wife." And then coming to the history of France—to this kingdom which, he says, is peculiarly that of Héloïse and himself: *regno praecipue nostro, id est Francorum*—he recalls how Clovis was converted not by the preaching of saints, but through the intercession of the queen, his

wife. And as he reflects in this manner, the thoughts of Abelard, who had likened himself to Cain, cursed to be a wanderer
and fugitive, turn back to the time he was at the Paraclete
after making it over to Héloïse—that haven where he would
gladly have found refuge from the tempest. He recalls the
prayers that were offered in the chapel, and bids Héloïse remember them too. Echoing with a slight variation words she
had used to him (*Nosti, charissime*) he writes: *Nosti, dilec-
tissime*—"You know, my beloved, with what a warmth of
charity your community sent up their prayers when I was
with you. For every day at the end of each of the Hours they
used to make this supplication to the Lord for me; and, the
response for the day and its versicle having been said and
sung, continued with these prayers and a collect:

Response: Forsake me not, O Lord; O my God, be not far
from me.

Versicle: Make haste, O God, to deliver me.

Prayer: Save thy servant, O my God, whose hope is in
thee.

Versicle: Lord, hear my prayer and let my cry come to
thee. (*let us pray*) God who through Thy servant has been pleased to gather thy handmaids
together in this place, we beseech thee that
thou wilt protect him from all adversity and
restore him in safety to his handmaidens.

Héloïse had asked Abelard to restore to her his presence.
In his involved manner he makes it plain that it is at the
Paraclete that he would choose to be. And if this is not possible during his life, then let it be so after his death. For if, he
continues, the Lord should deliver him into the hands of his
enemies and they prevail over him and kill him, then may his
body, wherever it lie, buried or unburied, be brought to rest at
the convent where the nuns looking each day at his tomb

may think to offer prayers on his behalf. For what better
resting place could there be than one consecrated to the Holy
Spirit, the Comforter, among women whose lives are dedicated to Christ? His thoughts turn again to the women of
the Scriptures: "Women kept watch at the tomb of the Lord
Jesus Christ; they came to it with precious ointments, they
went ahead and followed. They faithfully waited at the tomb
and mourned with tears the death of the Bridegroom, as it is
written 'the women sitting over against the tomb lamented
the Lord'. And there, before his Resurrection, they were comforted by the appearance and the words of an angel and
afterwards found worthy to taste of the joy of Christ's Resurrection—when he appeared to them twice—and to touch him
with their hands." On this note he brings his letter to a close,
wishing well to Héloïse and her sisters and asking that they
be mindful of him.

> Vive vale vivantque tuae valeantque sorores.
> Vivite in Christo, quaeso, mei memores.

[Life and health to you and to your sisters. And in your
lives remember me, I beg you, in Christ.]

THE FIRST LETTER FROM HÉLOÏSE TO ABELARD

translated from the Latin

To her master or rather father, to her husband or rather
brother; his handmaid or rather daughter, his wife or rather
sister: to Abelard, Héloïse.

Not long ago, my beloved, someone brought me by chance
your letter that you sent to a friend to comfort him. When I
saw at once from the superscription that it was yours, I began
to read the more eagerly because the writer is so dear to me,
hoping that the words would at least bring before me a picture

of him whose presence I have lost and thus console me. But almost every line of this letter was filled, I remember, with gall and wormwood, as it told the pitiful tale of our entry into religion and of the adversities that you, who are my all, bear without respite. You did indeed fulfil in that letter the promise made at the beginning to your friend that he would esteem his own trials as nothing or of little account as compared with yours. Having recalled first of all how your masters persecuted you, and then the maiming of your body through an act of supreme treachery, you went on to tell of the appalling venom and the violent onslaughts with which those fellow-students of yours, Alberic of Rheims and Lotulph of Lombardy, pursued you. You did not pass over what (at their prompting) was done to your glorious theological work; or what amounted to your imprisonment. You further described the plots made against you by your abbot and false brethren, and the calumnies, so distressing to you, of those two "false apostles", instigated by the former unworthy rivals. You told of the scandal in the eyes of many because, contrary to custom, you named your oratory the Paraclete. Finally, coming to the intolerable persecutions that you continue to endure at the present time, from that pitiless tyrant and the wicked monks you call your sons, you brought your unhappy story to its end. It is one, I think, which no one could read or hear without shedding tears. The detail in which you have told it has aroused in me a sorrow that is the greater because you say that your dangers are still growing—so that here we are driven one and all to despair of your life and each day we await in fear and trembling the news of your death.

And so in the name of Christ who still to some measure protects you for his service, we, his handmaids and yours, beg you to write constantly and tell us without fail of the tempests which continue to buffet you, so that we at least, who alone are left you, may share whether it be in your sorrow or

your joy. For in times of sorrow it is a comfort to know that
sorrow is shared. And a burden laid on several is borne more
easily, or even removed. And if this tempest shall have abated
for a little, you must hasten the more to send a letter, for it
will be the more welcome. But whatever you write to tell us,
you will confer on us no small favour, for you will show that
you have us in mind. How truly welcome is a letter from an
absent friend Seneca himself shows us by his own example,
when he writes in one passage to his friend Lucilius: "Thank
you for writing often, for by the one means that is possible
you put yourself in my presence. Never do I have a letter of
yours without our being immediately together. If pictures of
absent friends give us pleasure, if they refresh our memory and
assuage the pain of separation, though it be by a false and
empty solace, how much more welcome is a letter which sets
before us the very handwriting of the one who is far away."
Thanks be to God that at least in this no evil intent can
debar you, no difficulty prevent you, from restoring to me
your presence. I beg, then, let no negligence on your part
hold you back.

You wrote your friend a long letter, no doubt to console
him in his misfortunes, but telling about your own. In faithfully recording these for his comfort you have greatly added
to our distress. In your wish to heal his wounds you have
dealt us fresh wounds of grief, besides intensifying those that
were ours already. Heal, I beg you, the wounds you have yourself inflicted—you who are busy tending the wounds inflicted
by others. You have complied with the wishes of a friend and
a comrade; you have paid the debt of friendship and fellowship. Far more pressing is the debt you have incurred towards
us; for we are entitled to be called not only your friends but
your most dear friends; not only your comrades but your
daughters—unless you can think of a name more tender, more
holy. As to the magnitude of the debt by which you have

bound yourself to us there is lack neither of argument nor evidence, should proof be needed. Though the whole world were to keep silent, the fact itself cries aloud. For you alone after God are the founder of this place, you alone are the builder of this oratory, you alone the maker of this congregation. Nor have you built here on the foundation of another. All that is here is your own work. In this desolate spot once the haunt of wild creatures and robbers, which had never known human habitation, never contained a dwelling—here among the lairs of savage beasts and the hiding places of brigands, where God's name is not to be heard, you raised a sanctuary to the glory of God, dedicated a shrine to the Holy Spirit. To build it you did not draw on the wealth of kings or princes, though lavish wealth was there for the asking. Whatever was done, the credit was to be yours alone. Clerics and scholars, flocking here zealous for your teaching, provided all your needs. Even those who lived by ecclesiastical benefices, who did not know how to make an offering but only to receive one, whose hands were ready to take but not to give— even these came forward with generous contributions. It is yours, then, truly yours, this new plantation in the fields of the Lord. But the plants that are in it are still very young, they are in need of watering if they are to grow. And even if it were not new, this plantation would be weak—through the very weakness of woman's nature. For this reason it demands a more thorough and more attentive cultivation in accordance with the words of the Apostle: "I have planted, Apollos watered; but God gave the increase." The Apostle by the doctrine that he taught had planted and established in the faith the Corinthians to whom he was writing. Afterwards, Apollos, the Apostle's own disciple, had watered them with exhortations to holiness, and so it was that divine grace bestowed on them an increase in the virtues.

You cultivate the vineyard of another, which you did not

plant and which has turned to your own bitterness. Your admonitions are often fruitless, your sermons preached in vain. You who expend your care on another's vineyard, think what you owe to your own. You teach and admonish rebels, achieving nothing. In vain you cast before swine the pearls of your God-given eloquence. You who expend much thought on the obstinate, think what you owe to the obedient. You who shower gifts on your enemies, reflect how you are in-debted to your daughters. The others apart, think by how great a debt you have bound yourself to me—that what you owe to a community of women consecrated to God you may pay with greater devotion to her who is yours in a manner that is unique.

With your superior knowledge you know far better than do we in our nothingness, how many long and serious treatises the Fathers of the Church compiled for the instruction, the encouragement and even the consolation of women, and with what care they compiled these. And so since we in this community are but the first frail shoots that you planted, it is astonishing that all this time (so forgetful of us are you) neither out of reverence for God nor love of us nor to follow the example of the Fathers of the Church have you at-tempted either by word of mouth when you were here or by letter when away to comfort me, harassed as I am and crushed by prolonged grief. And yet you know that you are bound to me by a debt which is the greater because you are united to me in the bond of the marriage sacrament; and that you are the more beholden to me because I have loved you always, as all know, with a love to which I have set no limit. You know, my beloved, the whole world knows, by what a cruel stroke of fortune that most shameful, public act of treachery, in robbing me of you, robbed me of my very self; and that I grieve incomparably more for the manner in which I lost you than for the loss itself. The greater the cause of grief, the greater the need of solace. And this must come from none but you, since you, who are alone the cause of my grief, alone can confer the grace of solace. For it is you alone who can make me sad, make me joyful or comfort me. It is you alone who owes me this immense debt. All your orders I fulfilled—to such a degree that, unable to gainsay you in anything, I found strength at a word from you to bring ruin upon myself. More than that (it is a strange story) my love reached such a pitch of madness that it robbed itself beyond hope of recovery of what it most desired—when straightway at your bidding I changed both my manner of dress and my purpose to prove that you alone were the master of my body and soul alike. Nothing, God is my witness, have I ever sought in you other than yourself. You alone and not what was yours I desired. I did not look for the bond of marriage nor for any marriage-portion. It was not assuredly my own pleasures or wishes, as you yourself know, but yours that I sought to gratify. Though the title of wife be judged more holy and more binding, I always held more sweet the word mistress, or, if you will forgive me, concubine or whore. I thought that the more I humbled myself for your sake the greater favour I would win in your eyes; and that in this way I would tarnish less the splendour of your reputation. And you yourself did not entirely forget this in the letter I have mentioned which you wrote for the comfort of a friend. For in it you did not disdain to set out some of the arguments I used to try to dissuade you from our union in an ill-starred marriage. Yet you passed over in silence a number of my reasons for preferring love to marriage, freedom to a bond. I call God to witness that if Augustus, ruler of the entire world, had deemed fit to honour me with marriage and make over the whole earth for me to rule for ever, I would have been happier and thought it more seemly to be called your harlot than his empress. For a man's worth does not reside in riches or power. These are dependent on fortune, his worth on merit.

A woman should know that she is selling herself, who marries a rich man more readily than one who is poor; and who desires in her husband anything other than himself. Assuredly a woman who brings to her marriage covetousness such as this deserves payment not affection. For it is plain that she is thinking of her husband's income not of himself, and is ready, if she can, to prostitute herself to someone richer. This is the argument put forward (in the dialogue of Aeschines, pupil of Socrates) by the wise Aspasia to Xenophon and his wife, when after trying to bring about a reconciliation, she concludes with the words: "Only when you realise that there is not a better man or more lovable woman on earth will you always seek above all else what will seem to you the height of good fortune—you to be the husband of the best of wives, she to be the wife of the best of husbands." This is assuredly a happy saying and one that goes beyond philosophy—indeed it belongs to wisdom rather than to philosophy. For it is a holy error and a blessed fallacy among the married to suppose that true affection can keep the bonds of marriage unbroken not so much through continence of the body as through purity of heart.

But what error led the rest of women to hold, plain truth revealed to me; for what they clearly imagined about their husbands, I and the world at large not so much believed as knew to be true of yourself; so that my love for you was the more genuine in that it was the further removed from error. For what king or philosopher could match you in fame? What country, what city, what village did not long to see you? When you appeared in public, who, tell me, did not hurry to catch a glimpse of you? When you went away who did not turn to follow you with their gaze? What wife, what young girl did not long for you in your absence, burn in your pres-

ence? What queen or great lady did not envy me my joys
and my bed?

Moreover you had, I confess, two particular gifts by which
you could at once win the heart of any woman. You could
compose songs and sing them—and we know that other philosophers have rarely been able to do that. This was for you
in the nature of a diversion—a respite from your labours in
philosophy; and you left behind many love-songs and verses
which won wide popularity. The words and the tunes had
such charm that your name was continually on the lips of all
—so lovely were the airs that not even the unlettered were
allowed to forget you. This more than anything made women
sigh with love for you. And as the greater number of these
lyrics told of our love, they soon made my name widely
known and roused the jealousy of many women against me.

For what excellence of mind or body did not grace your
manhood? Among the women who then envied me is there
one now who is not compelled to feel compassion for me
robbed as I am of such happiness? Who is there, man or
woman, even though an enemy formerly, who is not moved
with a compassion that is my due? Exceedingly guilty, yet, as
you know, I am exceedingly innocent. For it is not the deed
but the intention that makes a crime. Justice weighs not what
is done but the spirit in which it is done. And what my attitude towards you has been only you who have knowledge of
it can judge. I submit all to your scrutiny; I yield all to your
testimony.

Tell me one thing, if you can—why, after our entry into
religion which you alone decided upon, am I so neglected, so
forgotten, that I have neither the encouragement of your
words and presence nor the consolation of a letter in your
absence? Tell me, I say, if you can. No, I will tell you what I
believe and what moreover all suspect. It was lust not affection that bound you to me, the heat of passion not love.

When, therefore, what you wanted ceased, all your show of tenderness vanished too. This, my beloved, is not merely my view but that of everyone. It is not a private but a general belief; not a personal sentiment but widely held. Would to God it were mine alone and that the love you profess could find someone to defend it, for that would comfort me a little. I only wish I could invent reasons to excuse you and in some measure conceal my dejection.

Listen, I beg you, to what I ask. You will see that it is a small favour and one that will cost you little. While I am robbed of your presence grant me at least through your words (these you have in plenty) the happiness of being with you. In vain can I hope to find you generous in deeds if you are niggardly in words. Up to now I had thought that I deserved much of you; for I have fulfilled all for your sake, persevering to this day only in obedience to you. It was not a vocation to the religious life but your bidding alone which made me submit as a young girl to the austerities of the cloister. If from you I deserve nothing, then my labour is indeed vain. For I can expect in return no reward from God, since it is certain that to this day I have done nothing for love of him. When you were hastening on your way to God I followed you. I did more, I went ahead. For remembering how Lot's wife looked back, you made me put on the religious habit and take my vows first, before you gave yourself to God. Your lack of trust in me in this one thing filled me, I must tell you, with the most bitter grief and shame. I would not have hesitated (God knows this) at your bidding to go before you or to follow you into the very flames of hell. For my heart was not with me, but with you. And now, more than ever, if it is not with you, it is nowhere. For in truth without you it cannot exist. But so act that it may be at rest with you, I beg you. And it will be at rest with you if it find you gracious; if you give kindness for kindness, a small return for a great, words for deeds.

Would that, my beloved, you had less confidence in my love for you, for then you would be more anxious on my behalf. But the more reason I have given you to feel confidence in me, the more neglectful do I find you. Remember, I entreat you, what I have done and consider the debt that you owe me. While I enjoyed with you the pleasures of the flesh, many wondered whether I acted from love or from passion. Now the end is proof of the beginning. I have denied myself all pleasures to obey your will. I have kept nothing for myself except to be now, more than ever, yours. Consider then your injustice if when I deserve more you give me less, indeed nothing at all, especially when it is a small favour I ask and one easy to grant.

And so in the name of God to whom you have dedicated yourself I beg you that, in such way as you can, you restore to me your presence; by writing me, that is, some word of consolation, that thus refreshed I may give myself more readily to God's service. When you sought me out long ago for worldly pleasures your letters came one upon another and your many songs set your Héloïse upon the lips of all. Every public place, every house echoed with my name. How much more fitting that you should incite me now towards God, than then to passion. Consider, I beg you, what you owe me. Give heed to what I ask. I close my long letter with a brief ending. Farewell, my all.

CHAPTER VI

"He for God only, she for God in him."

Milton

IN her previous superscription Héloïse had tried different forms of address, discarding one for another; master for father, husband for brother. Then, in the letter, she had used another word: *unicus*. She had ended: *Vale, unice*. "Farewell, my all." And now at the head of her second letter she writes: *Unico suo post Christum, unica sua in Christo*. "To him who is her all after Christ, she who is his all in Christ." Abelard had acknowledged her as his wife, but he had stressed that she was his sister in Christ, a religious with the obligations that devolve on such. This being so, her logical mind reflects, her first allegiance is to Christ. Hence she writes *unico post Christum*: "to her all after Christ". Not even Abelard the monk can take exception to that. But if he is her all; if she is dependent on him—as indeed she has already made clear not only in her words and manner of address, but in her insistence upon her need of him—the converse is true. She, no less, is his all. Where, except at the Paraclete has he a friend to whom he may turn? Abelard had addressed her as his "sister in Christ", and she accepts this. But she would remind him that this is only one facet of the truth. As a religious she belongs to Christ, but to Abelard she is more than a sister. The fact of her belonging to Christ does not diminish the degree in which she belongs to Abelard. That as an act of obedience to her husband she chose to give herself to Christ in religion, is the supreme proof, if one were needed, that she belongs in very truth to Abelard.

In the letter that follows there is no trace of her previous indignation. The tone is one of tender concern for Abelard, coupled with a renewed appeal for his help. Her writing is deeply emotional, yet, as she looks back to the past, she does not lapse into vain repinings. She recalls lost happiness with a nostalgia that is devoid of sentimentality. The fact that, however violent her feelings, her intellect remains in command, gives to the writing of Héloïse a vigour and an astringency. She knows not only what it is she wants to say, but her purpose in saying it. In her first letter she had shown her awareness of Abelard's mood of despondency by urging him to cease attempting at Saint-Gildas what he could not hope to achieve; instead, to give his mind to the task awaiting him in his own foundation of the Paraclete. He had responded to this to some degree. He had said that, if she wished, he was ready to write to her on spiritual matters. He had also said that he would send the promised psalter, and had enclosed prayers to be offered on his behalf. Nevertheless his preoccupation had been with himself, his troubles, and the possibility of his death. He had shown little concern for her. Héloïse does not comment on this. Instead, she throws out not so much questions as provocative statements designed to call for a response and thus rouse Abelard from his self-absorption.

She is amazed, she says (not without irony), that in the wording of his superscription he has reversed the convention observed in the heading of letters, in that he has put her name in front of his own, Héloïse before Abelard. What can he have been thinking about, to give a woman precedence over a man, a wife over a husband, a servant over a master, a nun over a monk, an abbess over an abbot? That she should mention this points to the fact that, having been indignant with Abelard in her previous letter, she wants him to know that she does nevertheless esteem him above herself. But there is more than this in her mind. She must have realised that Abelard, in reversing the order of address, was expressing his regard for her—it was all the more obvious because he had devoted a large part of his letter to the praise of women. Even so, if such was his intention, Héloïse would have him be yet more explicit. After all, it was not so long ago that she had read in the *Historia Calamitatum* his plea to Fulbert that women since the beginning of time had caused the downfall of great men. And how much this was in her thoughts is revealed presently when, taking up the same point, she dwells on it at length.

Héloïse expresses further amazement that, when she had asked Abelard for comfort, he had increased her distress first by his words (which she quotes) towards the end of his letter: "If the Lord should deliver me into the hands of my enemies", and then, following this, his request that, should he die, his body be brought to the Paraclete. "My beloved," she exclaims, "what made you think such a thought, how could you bear to put it into words?" *O carissime, quo id animo cogistasti, quo id ore dicere sustinuisti?* She had, it is true, begged him for news good or bad, but when she hears to what dangers he is exposed and that his death may be imminent, this is more than she can bear. She had been anxious already, fearing, as she had said, that each day would bring to the Paraclete news of his death. Abelard's letter had done nothing to allay her anxiety. Moreover, distressing as it is to learn that a loved-one is in danger, this distress diminishes or increases in accordance with what is known to be that person's state of mind. To know that such a one is, in spite of all, in good heart is itself a reassurance; whereas to see Abelard, as Héloïse saw him, downcast and discouraged, was an added anxiety. Her nerves frayed, her imagination running riot, she evokes the scene of desolation at the Paraclete should he lose his life. She hears the mourning and weeping. He has asked for prayers for his soul, but that, she does not hesitate to tell him, will be no time for prayer when all are prostrate with grief. Besides, the thought of being finally separated from him who gives purpose to her life is beyond endurance. If he is gone what hope is left? Who will be at hand to heal her sorrow? As it is, the fact that he is alive is her sole conso- lation—were he to die she would lose not him alone, but her very self. Héloïse was not by nature a Stoic. She read and ad- mired the Stoic writers of ancient Rome: Seneca, Lucan, Persius were all familiar to her. She was steeped in Saint Jerome, who in some respects was as much a Stoic as a Chris- tian. She found inspiration in these writers and sought in ad- versity to mould herself to a pattern of behaviour that would have been acceptable in their eyes. But she was doing violence to herself. At Argenteuil on the day of her profession she had gone to the altar with Lucan's verses on her lips, but not all her resolution could hold back her tears. And now again she is quoting Lucan, bidding Abelard take to heart the poet's prayer that death, when it comes, may come suddenly; that the mind be not burdened in advance by dark and useless fears. Let Abelard stop thinking of death, if not for his own sake then for hers.

One motive can dovetail into another. Héloïse asked Abe- lard for help because she was entitled to it, needed it and wanted it. She wanted his help to enable her to live the life to which she was committed for his sake. Moreover, shut away at the Paraclete, she needed contact with a mind as intelli- gent as her own. She also wanted his help because she wanted Abelard himself; and this was a means, the only means now open, by which she could be united to him. In revealing the thoughts of her heart, yet in doing so through the medium of a religious speaking to her father in Christ, she is assuring him in imagery, the underlying meaning of which not even the dull-witted could fail to understand, of her unchanging devotion to him who, despite altered circumstances, is still

her husband. But this is not all. In laying bare her need of
him, she is reiterating what she had told him in her first
letter, when she urged him to abandon Saint-Gildas for his
own foundation—that, however it may be elsewhere, here at
the Paraclete obligations await him which he is duty-bound
to fulfil. In her twofold capacity, as his wife and at the same
time his daughter in Christ, she appeals to him. Yes, she is
his wife; and through his dispensation, not that of God, she
is the abbess of the Paraclete.

It was not the nature of Héloïse to be submissive. She
would like to cry out against the cruelty of God. "Would
that it were not blasphemy to say: 'O God cruel to me in all
things.'" *O si fas sit dici; crudelem mihi per omnia Deum.*
And having thus apostrophised God, or given voice to a wish
to do so, she drops into the language and imagery of classical
Rome, remonstrating not with the God of Christianity, but
with the goddess Fortune, for having expended against her
all the arrows that her quiver holds. The happiness she once
had known makes her present lot the more desperate. Yet
what hurts her most, because it affronts her sense of justice,
is not her own fate but that of Abelard. While their love had
been illicit, God had spared them. But scarcely had they made
amends, exchanged fornication for marriage, than God must
needs lift his hand against not both of them but Abelard,
punishing him in a manner meted out in cases of the most
flagrant adultery. What adulteresses have brought upon their
lovers, his own wife—this is what Héloïse cannot forgive
either herself or God—brought upon Abelard.

It is here that, recalling Abelard's plea to Fulbert that
women from the beginning of time have destroyed great men,
she takes this up, not to deny it, but to enlarge upon it, citing
instance after instance from the Scriptures and leaving Abelard to draw his conclusions and to answer. She accepts responsibility (that is what she is telling him) for the mutila-

tion. It was the consequence of her having allowed herself to be persuaded into the marriage; and, to make this worse, it was perpetrated through the agency of her uncle. Does Abelard (she is asking) really—as distinct from putting this forward as an excuse for his own weakness—see her as one of the women whom he had in mind when he made his plea to Fulbert? Let him tell her. He has grounds for thinking so, and yet (her sense of justice is again affronted) is he being fair? Reiterating a point made in her first letter, she maintains that this at least she can claim, that unlike the women she has cited—unlike Delilah, who caused Samson in ruining his enemies to bring ruin on himself—she, Héloïse, was not guilty in intent. Her guilt came not of any will to do wrong, but of an excess of love. And in saying this she is confirming what Abelard says in the *Historia Calamitatum*, that she married him because she could not bear to offend him in anything. Yet, though she argues thus, her probing mind, content with nothing less than the truth, cannot let it rest at this. For if in consenting to the marriage there had been no evil intent but solely the desire to do what was best for Abelard, there had been "many wrongdoings beforehand" (*peccata tamen multa praecesserunt*) for which the sequel comes as a fitting punishment, in that "evil beginnings find issue in an untoward end". Sin demands expiation. Willingly she would pass a lifetime of expiation, if in so doing she could atone, in contrition of heart, to Abelard, if not to God.

Here Héloïse comes to the heart of her letter, confronting Abelard with the falseness of her position as a religious—the discrepancy between appearance and reality. Yes, it is to Abelard to whom she would make reparation: to Abelard not to God. For how can she hope, she asks, to appease God, whom she charges, if not in word yet in the depths of her heart, with the utmost cruelty by reason of the outrage done to Abelard? She can only offend God, rebellious as she is against his ordinance. Moreover what kind of repentance is it when, however severe the mortification endured in the body, the mind retains, as does hers, the will to do wrong: *si mens adhuc ipsam retinet voluntatem?* It is an easy matter to confess faults, accuse oneself, make outward satisfaction—yet to what purpose if the heart clings to its former desires? The pleasures she once enjoyed with Abelard cannot, merely because time has passed, become displeasing to her. Nor, except with the greatest difficulty, can she erase them from her memory. They are there always, waiting to confront her. In sleep they haunt her dreams. During the sacrifice of the Mass they make prayer a mockery. She should be lamenting her past—instead, she is sighing for what she has lost. The very hours that she spent in Abelard's company, the places where they were together, all are graven on her memory, torturing her with a longing for what is no more. Her whole being cries out against a way of life alien to her nature. In one respect Abelard, despite his misfortunes, is blessed as compared with herself: cruel though the mutilation was, it cured him, at one stroke, of longings which pursue her unceasingly. God, after all, has shown himself propitious to him, a good physician who inflicts pain only to heal. This is not an empty complaint. Héloïse is determined that Abelard, downcast as he is, shall know that he is as dear to her as he once was; that the religious life has provided for her no escape, no substitute for what she has lost in losing him. She became a religious for him, without a vocation; he must not suppose that in the meanwhile a vocation has presented itself. He must know what she believes to be the truth, for his sake as well as for hers.

She has won praise in the sight of men, who, failing to discern the true person behind the façade of the nun, commend her chastity, making the purity of the flesh into a virtue when it is a virtue not of the body, but of the mind. Man is deceived, but not God who sees into the heart. Such deception, she maintains, is to be expected in an age in which religion is tainted with hypocrisy—one in which those win esteem who find favour in the sight of men. Yet, for a moment, she asks herself if she may not take comfort in the thought that, at least in outward demeanour, she has not given scandal to the Church or shamed the habit she wears. Is it not a virtue of a kind to abstain from evil? But Héloïse is not one to be content with half-measures. "Depart from evil", the Scriptures say, "and do good." Yet the former avails nothing if the latter does not follow. And both are vain if not done for love of God.

In simple words Héloïse states her case to Abelard and asks his help. The help she asks of him he must not depute to another, not even though the other be God. She had told him in her previous letter that he alone could make her sad, he alone make her joyful or comfort her. She is not asking to escape from the religious life. What she is telling him is that she needs, indeed must have, his help if she is to persevere to the end. Having done nothing for God, she is entitled neither to help nor reward from God. "At every stage of my life, God knows, up to the present, I have feared to offend you rather than God, sought to please you rather than him. Your bidding and not any love of God made me put on the habit of religion. Reflect, then, what an unhappy life I must lead—one that is miserable beyond all others—if I endure this in vain with no hope of reward in the future."

Out of devotion to Abelard, with all the strength of her will and with a Stoic courage, Héloïse played the role required of her—first at Argenteuil, then as abbess of the Paraclete. But in doing this she has, she declares, misled not only others but Abelard himself—so deceived him (his praise of her, she tells him, is evidence of this) as to make him suppose she has no need of his help, so that instead of praying for her he is asking for her prayers. Let him not presume so highly of her, lest thinking her strong he fail her when she is most in need. She wants not flattery but help—help in the form of an assurance that Abelard has her welfare at heart; an assurance, too, that what she has done for him, and is doing, does not go unnoticed.

Her words are gentle and persuasive. But do they contain a hidden warning? She asks that he be anxious on her account, rather than confident—that she may be helped by the knowledge of his concern. He has, she says, the more reason for anxiety, now that she no longer has in him a refuge from her own passionate nature. If he shows himself indifferent to her; if he takes for granted the fidelity that she has preserved towards him not easily, but with a struggle and in despite of her own nature, will she remain faithful to him? Is this the question that she is putting into his mind—to rouse him by yet another means from his pre-occupation with self? To conceive of her as unfaithful to Abelard is to postulate an Héloïse inconsistent with all that is known of her from her writings and those of her contemporaries. Héloïse had no intention of being unfaithful. A warning or threat can be a device (sometimes an unconscious one) to bring home with particular vividness a point that might else pass unnoticed. Héloïse is asking Abelard not to try her beyond endurance.

When arguing against the marriage, Héloïse had held up the ideal of the celibate cleric-philosopher, either because she genuinely believed that Abelard's proper place was among the giants of the spiritual life, as exemplified by Saint Jerome, or because she knew that Abelard who, not content unless in a blaze of glory, would be dissatisfied were he to be excluded from this company. For herself, she has no such ambitions. She does not think of herself in terms of heroism, spiritual or otherwise. If God will grant her but a "corner in heaven" he will be doing enough: *Quocunque me angulo coeli Deus col-*

locet, satis mihi faciet. And she gives her reason—that in
heaven none will envy another, since each soul will have
what will suffice for itself. Héloïse asks of God the degree of
happiness to which her devotion to Abelard will entitle her.
Were she to love Abelard less she would not love God more
—she would no longer be true to herself, and so, far from
winning a victory, she would suffer a defeat. Supporting her
argument with a quotation from Saint Jerome, she asks why
should she abandon what is sure for that which is unsure?

Sponsae Christi servus eiusdem. [To the bride of Christ,
the servant of the same.] The superscription to Abelard's
reply is itself an answer to the question put by Héloïse as to
why he had placed her name before his own. He goes on to
elaborate this. He is in agreement with her that, when writing to a superior, it is customary for the name of the latter to
appear first. Héloïse, he says, has been his superior since the
day when she was raised from being the bride of a man to
become the bride of Christ. In thus addressing her he is
following the example of Saint Jerome: "For this reason I
write 'my lady' Eustochium, for I must call her 'my lady' who
is the bride of my Lord." And so, reverting to a theme he had
touched on in his previous letter, Abelard continues: "Do not
marvel if I commend myself both alive and dead to your
prayers, since it is established by common law that with their
lords wives prevail more than do the rest of the household,
being ladies rather than slaves. As a type of such the queen
and bride of the King of Kings is described, where it is written
in the psalm: 'Upon my right hand did stand the queen.'"
Abelard goes on to cite the Ethiopian woman whom Moses
took to wife: "I am black but I am beautiful, daughters of
Jerusalem. Therefore the king has loved me and brought me
into his chamber." *Nigra sum sed formosa, filiae Hierusalem.
Ideo dilexit me rex et introduxit me in cubiculum suum.* As

he writes of the Ethiopian woman, Abelard's thoughts are
close to Héloïse; he has in mind the "black, coarse" habit
which she will wear to the end of her life for his sake. But
the black, as was that of the Ethiopian woman, is on the
exterior. "She is black in what is without but inwardly
comely": *nigra itaque in exterioribus sed formosa in interiori-
bus est.* To console Héloïse he stresses inner beauty, inner
glory: the king's daughter is glorious within. Preferring as always the secret to the open, the abstruse to the obvious, he
reflects on variations of this theme. Rightly, he maintains,
does the Ethiopian say that, because she is black and comely,
for that reason she is beloved and taken into the chamber of
the king.

Abelard sees the letter he has received from Héloïse as
falling under four headings, and replies accordingly. After giving his reasons for putting her name before his own, he answers her complaint that far from consoling her he has,
through dwelling on the possibility of his death, added to her
distress. He told her, he explains, of the dangers to which he
was exposed only because she had asked him to do so. Had
she not written begging him in the name of Christ to tell his
servants at the Paraclete, the only friends left to him, of his
perils and afflictions? Had she not said that sympathy
awaited him? Why, then, does she complain, when he has
done as she asked? Abelard is logical, but he shows a lack of
imagination. It is one thing to be prepared for bad news, another to face it or its near certainty with equanimity. What
Abelard takes as a reproach—interpreting the words of Héloïse
at their face value and not discerning the implication—is on
her part an expression of solicitude and love. Héloïse had
begged for his presence—that is, his veritable presence or, if
not that, a letter; she was not prepared to be offered his dead
body.

Speaking as might a confessor to a penitent (is this a mask

to conceal, from himself as much as from her, a deeper, more personal concern; or has the role of monk become second nature?) he commends her disinclination to be praised. This, he says, if it is genuine, is a proof of her humility. But is it genuine? She must ask herself. There would be something offensive in the manner in which Abelard probes the conscience of Héloïse, were this not counterbalanced by a lightness of touch in his sudden incursion into Virgil's story of the nymph Galatea hiding in the willow-beds, not to conceal herself from her pursuer, but to attract his attention. Did a smile light the face of Abelard as he wrote:

Et fugit ad salices et se cupit ante videri,

[She darted into the willows hoping first to be seen.]?

Is that, he asks, what Héloïse is doing, darting away under cover of self-effacement, yet hoping to attract attention? Letters, particularly those that belong to a past remote from that of the reader, raise a problem. A poem or essay or a narrative intended (as is normally the case) for a general public, though it does not disclose the full depth of its meaning to every reader, is to a greater or lesser degree self-explanatory. In a letter, on the other hand, written usually to be read by one person, words can have a private meaning and carry with them associations intelligible only to those immediately concerned. We cannot know what Virgil's words evoked in the mind of Héloïse—what memory going back to the days when she and her tutor were reading the classics in the house in the rue des Chantres.

He passes on to the fourth part of the letter, to what he calls "that longstanding persistent complaint": *antiquam illam et assiduam querimoniam*, wherein, concerning their joint entry into religion, she blames God when, according to Abelard, she ought to praise him. There is in his words the exasperation of one who writes under a strain. Why (this is the implication) must she revert to the past? He wants to forget it. It was indeed necessary to his peace of mind that he should forget. In the religious life he had found justification: he could see himself as a brand snatched from the fire. Why cannot Héloïse do the same? Why cannot she see in the mutilation and what followed—in her own life no less than in his—the hand of God? He had hoped, he continues, that what he calls her "bitterness of heart", *amaritudinem animi*, provoked by what had transpired to be an act of divine mercy, had vanished; a bitterness wearisome to her body no less than to her soul, and grievous to him as well as to herself. Let her, then, once and for all lay this aside, for his sake—that she may not cause him torment. Unable to face the situation for which he is responsible, Abelard wants to be reassured, to be told that all is well. And so he places the onus on her. "With this [that is, her present attitude of mind] you can neither please me nor attain with me to blessedness."

One can forgive him for what amounts to emotional black-mail only because at this point a warmth (the more welcome because rare) infuses his words as he begs her to change her attitude and to unite herself with him: "Will you leave me to go on my way without you, you who boast that you are ready to follow me into the fires of hell? For this reason, if for none other, be true to your religious vocation, that you may not be cut off from me while I hasten, as you believe, on my way to God." If she will but unite herself with him, a happy fellowship is theirs, a happy goal awaits them.

Héloïse, though she reproached God for permitting the mutilation, had yet conceded that Providence had been kind to Abelard. He fastens on this point, developing it in an endeavour to show that her indignation is unfounded. She had blamed herself for being the cause, though unwittingly, of ill to Abelard. On the contrary, he argues, she has been the cause

of good. And here a naïve egoism prompts him to claim that
it was primarily for this end (that is, for his salvation) that
Héloïse had been created. He argues, too, that the punishment was a just one. Had they not, during the period of
separation after the marriage, desecrated (when he visited
her at Argenteuil), through the excess of his passion, a place
consecrated to the Virgin? And what of all that had preceded
the marriage? Not only the fornication, but the betrayal on
his part, whereby he had turned her uncle away from her. And
then, at the time of her pregnancy, she had used the religious
habit as a disguise when travelling to Brittany—was it not
fitting, therefore, that she should make reparation by wearing,
as a true religious, the habit of a nun? Has she forgotten, too,
the lengths to which they went in the early days of their love
—when they respected not even the holy season of the Passion; when, if she resisted, he forcibly constrained her? If she
will but think, she will see that God has been not only just
but merciful. Again a warmth and an urgency come into his
words: "Reflect, reflect, my beloved, how with the drag-nets
of his mercy the Lord has rescued us out of so perilous a sea,
from what a yawning Charybdis he has saved us, though it be
against our will." If Héloïse has shared in the wrong-doing,
she shares no less in the redemption, since they are bound,
the one to the other, by an inviolable bond: "Approach then,
my inseparable companion, in a common thanksgiving—you
who have shared alike in the fault and in the grace of pardon.
For of your salvation the Lord is not unmindful. Indeed he
has you ever in mind. By your name that echoes his, he
marked you as belonging to him when he called you Héloïse
after the name Heloim which is his own. He, I say, in his mercy
has resolved to succour two in one, two whom in one Satan
strove to destroy." It is through the marriage that they are
one; and he had married her, he tells her, because he had
loved her and wanted her for his own: "Only a short time

before this [that is, the mutilation] befell us, God had bound us mutually in the indissoluble bond of the marriage sacrament, when I desired to keep for myself for all time you whom I loved beyond measure." God, then, has used both the marriage and the mutilation as means of drawing the two of them to himself.

Abelard would have her reflect how her present lot, far from being one to be deplored, is above that of ordinary women. Instead of children born to the world, she bears in her wisdom spiritual children to the Lord; and hands which else would have been busy with domestic tasks turn the pages of the Scriptures. Let her then not be distressed. Whom the Lord loveth he chasteneth. This punishment is transitory, not eternal. It is one of purgation, not damnation. He begs her to turn her thoughts to Christ her Lord, who loves her as he, Abelard, has never loved her—to the Son of God, taken into the hands of evil men, led away, scourged, blindfold, mocked, buffeted, spat upon, crowned with thorns, hanging upon a cross; "Think of him, my sister, as your true spouse and the spouse of all the Church. Keep him in your mind. Keep your eyes upon him as he goes his way to be crucified, bearing his cross. Be one of the crowd, one of the women who weep and mourn for him." And again: "Have compassion on him who suffered willingly for your redemption and look with compunction on him who was crucified for you." Here we see the raw material on which Abelard was to draw for his hymn for Good Friday (*In Parasceve Domini, III Nocturno*), in which the spectators of the Crucifixion are asked to compassionate with him who, himself guiltless, takes guilt away. The hymn ends with a prayer that those who have shared in the suffering may have grace to laugh for joy on Easter day:

ut risum tribuas paschalis gratiae.

The letter, too, has a joyful ending. Héloïse is the bride of Christ; and Abelard, as well as being her husband, is her servant. He places his salvation into her hands; and in doing so exalts her above himself. She had said that she had no wish to fight for victory. He will have none of this. His glory must decrease, hers increase. It is her part to do battle for both of them. If it be the onslaughts of passion, he, since the mutilation, has no such battle to fight. This is left to her alone. And if the battle is hers, so is the crown. A prayer that Héloïse is to say on behalf of them both brings the letter to a close on a note of hope and joy, eulogising marriage and the role predestined for Héloïse and himself:

"God, who at the creation of the human race didst, in fashioning woman from a rib of man, sanctify the great mystery of the nuptial union; who didst confer the highest honour on marriage by being thyself born in wedlock and by performing thy first miracle at the wedding-feast at Cana; thou who didst grant in such manner as pleased thee this refuge for my frail and passionate nature, despise not the prayer which I thy humble servant pour out in supplication before the face of thy majesty by reason of my own excesses and those of my beloved. Pardon, O most merciful God (thou who art mercy itself), pardon our offences many and great as they are, and let the immensity of thy boundless mercy be measured to the multitude of our faults. Punish the guilty now, I beseech thee, that thou mayest spare them hereafter. Punish them in time that thou mayest spare them in eternity. Raise against thy servants the rod of correction, not the sword of wrath. Afflict their flesh that thou mayest save their souls. Come as a redeemer, not an avenger; as the God of mercy, not of justice; as a compassionate father, not a stern lord. Prove us, Lord, and try us, in the manner in which the prophet would have thee deal with him: 'Test me, Lord, put me to the proof: assay my utmost desires and thoughts'—that is, consider first my strength and measure out accordingly the burden of my temptations. This is the promise Saint Paul made to the faithful when he said: 'God will not play you false; he will not al-

low you to be tempted beyond your powers. With the temptation itself he will ordain the issue of it; he will enable you to
hold your own.' Thou, Lord, hast brought us together; thou
hast parted us, when and as was pleasing to thee. The work
that thou hast mercifully begun complete now in the multitude of thy mercy; and those whom thou hast parted for a
time in this world, unite forever in the next, thou who art our
hope, our heritage, our expectation, our consolation, Lord
blest for ever. Amen."

THE SECOND LETTER FROM HÉLOÏSE TO ABELARD

translated from the Latin

To him who is her only beloved after Christ, she who is his
alone in Christ.

I am surprised, my only beloved, that contrary to the custom observed in writing letters, contrary to the natural
order, you have thought fit, in the greeting that heads your
letter, to put my name before your own, woman before man,
wife before husband, servant before master, nun before monk
and priest, deaconess before abbot. The accepted and fitting
order is surely that those who write to superiors or equals
should put the name of these before their own; whereas in
writing to inferiors those taking precedence in rank take
precedence in the order of address. We were also greatly surprised that, instead of bestowing on us the balm of comfort,
you have increased our desolation, causing tears to flow when
you should have wiped them away. For who among us could
hear with dry eyes the words you wrote at the end of your
letter where you said: "But if the Lord shall deliver me into
the hands of my enemies so that they prevail over me and
slay me," and the rest? My beloved, what made you think

such a thought? How could you bear to put it into words? May God never so forget his humble servants as to let them outlive you. May he never grant to us a life that would be more grievous to bear than any kind of death. It is for you to perform the last rites over us, commend our souls to God and send ahead of you those whom you have gathered into his service—that you may no longer be troubled on our account but, in coming after us, be the happier because free of solicitude for our salvation.

Spare us, I beg you, master, spare us words of this kind which only make those already unhappy utterly so. Do not take away from us, before death, the source of our existence. "Sufficient unto the day is the evil thereof." That day, wrapped about with every kind of bitterness, will bring with it for all whom it shall find here enough distress. For "To what purpose is it," Seneca says, "to summon evil in advance and to destroy life before death has come?"

You ask, my only beloved, that, if you are doomed to end your life far from here, we shall have your body brought to our burial place, that, our thoughts continually set on you, you may reap a richer harvest in our prayers. But how do you imagine your memory could ever fade from among us? Besides, what time will that be for prayer, when excess of grief will allow us no tranquillity? When the soul will have lost the power of reason, the tongue the use of speech? When the mind distraught instead of at rest will, if I may so speak, rage against God and provoke him with complaints instead of appeasing him with supplications? Then in our sorrow it will be left for us only to lament—we shall not be able to pray. We shall be hastening to follow, not to bury you—we shall be more fitted to be laid in the grave ourselves than to lay you in yours. In losing you we shall have lost our life. If you leave us, we shall not be able to live. May we not survive to see that day! If the mention of your death is death to us, what will be the reality, if it finds us living? Never, God grant, may we survive to pay you that debt—to render you that service which we await from you. In this may we go before, not follow you. And so, I beg you, spare us. Spare her who is especially yours. Cease to use words wherewith you pierce our hearts as with swords of death, so that what comes before death is more grievous than death itself.

A heart overwhelmed with grief knows not calm. A mind beset with anxiety cannot devote itself sincerely to God. Do not, I pray you, hinder God's service to which you have especially committed us. May bitter grief, if come it must, come suddenly—that should be our prayer, that it may not torment us long beforehand with vain dread which no foresight can relieve. This is what the poet means when he prays to God:

> *Sit subitum quodcunque paras; sit caeca futuri*
> *Mens hominum fati; liceat sperare timenti.*

[Whatever thou hast in store, may it be sudden. Let the mind of man be blind to what the future holds. Permit our fears to hope.]

But what have I to hope for, if you are gone? What purpose to prolong this pilgrimage on which I have no support save in you—and none in you save the knowledge that you live? For I am denied all pleasure in you, debarred even your presence which at least from time to time could restore me to myself.

O God cruel to me in all things! Would it were not blasphemy to speak so! O mercy that knows no mercy! O fortune that is ill-fortune! For already fortune has spent against me all the shafts that are hers, so that she has none left with which to vent her wrath on others. She has exhausted against me the fulness of her quiver. Henceforth others have no cause to fear her onslaught. And if any weapon had still been hers, it would find in me no place in which to deal a wound. And yet, despite these many wounds, she has one fear, that death may end my torments; and though she does not cease to ruin me she fears the ruin that she hastens. Among unhappy women I am the most unhappy; among the unfortunate, the most unfortunate. To such a height was I lifted, when I was chosen before all others by you, that my fall, when I was flung down, brought the greater suffering to you and to myself alike. For the higher one is raised the heavier the fall. Among great and noble women was there one whom Fortune set above myself or raised to a like degree? Whom else has she so cast down, so crushed with grief? In you what glory she shed upon me! In you what ruin she has brought me! Violent in either extreme, she has observed moderation neither in good nor ill. To make me the most wretched of women she first made me happier than any—that, as I remembered what once was mine, my grief might match in intensity the ill-fortune that overtook me; that my regret for what I had lost might be no less than had been the joy of possession; that ecstasy might find its counterpart in despair.

To heighten my indignation at the outrage you suffered, in our case the laws of justice have been overturned. For while we enjoyed the pleasures of unbridled love, while we surrendered ourselves to fornication (pardon this shameful word, but it is precise) God's severity spared us. But when we had corrected what is unlawful by what is lawful, covered the shame of fornication by an honourable marriage, it was then that the Lord in his wrath made his hand to fall upon us, nor would he who had long suffered an unchaste union allow one that was chaste. The punishment that you suffered was one adequate for men taken in flagrant adultery. What others merit through adultery, you incurred through a marriage by which you were confident you had now made amends for all your wrong-doing. What adulterous women have brought upon their lovers, your own wife brought upon you. And this was not when, as formerly, we were given over to our pleasures, but when we were now temporarily apart, you directing the schools in Paris; I, at your command, living among the nuns at Argenteuil. When we were thus separated that we might devote ourselves, you the more zealously to the schools and I more freely to prayer and the study of the Scriptures—it was then, when we were living a life that was chaste and holy, that you alone in your body paid the penalty for what we had both alike committed. You alone were punished, though we were both at fault. You, who were less to blame, bore all. For you had made more than due reparation in humbling yourself for my sake and in lifting me up and with me all my family, so that you were less deserving of punishment, in the sight both of God and those traitors.

Unhappy am I indeed to have been born into the world to cause such wickedness! Must women always, then, be the ruin of great men? Hence in *Proverbs* the warning to beware of woman: "Hearken unto me now therefore, O ye children, and attend to the ways of my mouth. Let not thine heart decline to her ways, go not astray in her paths. For she hath cast down many wounded; yea, many strong men have been slain by her. Her house is the way to hell, going down to the chambers of death." And in *Ecclesiastes*: "I applied mine heart to know, and I found more bitter than death the woman, whose heart is snares and nets, and her hands as bands; who so pleaseth God shall escape from her; but the sinner shall be taken by her." At the beginning of the world woman banished man from Paradise; and she who had been created by the Lord as a helpmate for man became the instrument of his downfall. And that powerful man of God, the Nazarite whose conception was announced by an angel, Delilah alone overcame; it was she who betrayed him to his enemies, deprived him of his sight and drove him to such despair that, in bringing down ruin upon his enemies, he brought ruin upon himself. And Solomon, the wisest of all men, a woman alone, whom he had taken to himself, infatuated; and she drove him to such a pitch of madness that she plunged him whom the Lord had chosen to build his temple (in preference to David his father, who was a righteous man) into idolatry until the end of his life, so that he forsook the service of God which he had proclaimed and taught in his words and writings. Job, a most holy man, fought his last and hardest battle against his wife who was urging him to curse God. One thing the cunning tempter knew well from repeated experience, that the ruin of men is accomplished most easily through their wives. And so directing his usual malice against us also, he attacked by means of marriage him whom he could not overthrow by fornication. Not permitted to effect evil by means of evil, he effected evil through what is good.

I thank God for this at least, that the tempter did not persuade me to do evil of my own consent, as he did the women of whom I have spoken—though he turned my love into a cause of evil-doing. Yet if my heart be purged through innocence and I did not consent to the guilt of this crime, even so many sins went before which do not leave me wholly without blame. For yielding long before to the delights of carnal pleasure, I myself merited then what I now suffer. The sequel is a fitting punishment for my previous sins. Evil beginnings find an untoward end. For this offence, above all, I ask strength to do fit penance, especially that I may be able in some measure to make amends by long contrition for the pain of the wound inflicted on you—that what you endured in the body for a passing hour I may suffer, as is right, all my life in contrition of heart and thus make reparation to you at least, if not to God.

For if I am to admit to the weakness of my unhappy soul,

I know of no penance by which to appease God, whom by reason of that outrage I accuse always of the utmost cruelty. Rebelling against his ordinance I anger him by my indignation instead of appeasing him by repentance. For what kind of repentance is it, however great the mortification of the body, if the mind still retains the will to sin and burns with its old desires? It is easy to accuse oneself, confess one's sins, or even mortify the body by means of penance from without. But it is very hard to tear from the heart its longing for supreme pleasures. And it is with reason that Job, a saintly man, after saying: "I will leave my complaint upon myself," that is, "I will let loose my tongue and open my mouth in confession to accuse myself of my sins," straightway adds: "I will speak in the bitterness of my soul." Commenting on this, Saint Gregory says: "There are some who confess their faults aloud yet in confession do not know how to mourn, who speak cheerfully of what should be lamented." Thus is it that "Whoever hates his sins and declares them, must declare them in bitterness of heart, that this very bitterness may punish him for the deeds of which his tongue, prompted by the mind, accuses him." This bitterness which belongs to true repentance is rare, as Saint Ambrose remarks when he says: "I have found more easily those who have preserved their innocence than those who have repented." Indeed, so sweet to me were those delights that we enjoyed together as lovers, that I cannot despise them nor can I efface them, except with the greatest difficulty, from my memory. Wherever I turn they are there; and so is my longing for them. Not even in sleep am I spared their illusions. During the solemn moments of the Mass, when prayer should be the more pure, their unclean vision takes such complete possession of my unhappy soul that my thoughts are set on their vileness rather than on prayer. When I ought to be lamenting what I have done, I sigh for what I have lost.

And it is not only what we did, the very places and moments we shared are so graven on my mind that I live the past over again in your company. Not even in sleep have I respite. Sometimes my thoughts are betrayed by a movement of my body; or they reveal themselves in an unguarded word. Unhappy am I indeed. Well may I utter the complaint of a stricken soul: "O wretched that I am! Who shall deliver me from the body of this death?" I wish I could add with truth what follows: "I thank God through Jesus Christ Our Lord." This grace, my most beloved, came to you unsought; when, in healing you from these torments by a single wound to your body, it healed many wounds in your soul. God who seemed to be cruel to you is proved to have been kind. He is the good physician who does not shrink from causing pain if it is to heal. For me it is harder: I am young and passionate and I have known the most intense pleasures of love—and the attacks directed against me are the fiercer in that my nature is frail.

They say that I am chaste, not discerning the hypocrite in me. They turn the purity of the flesh into a virtue, when it is a virtue not of the body but of the soul. I win some praise among men, yet merit none in the sight of God who tries the heart and the reins and seeks out the hidden places. I am thought religious in this age in which there is little religion that is not tainted with hypocrisy—one in which whoever does not offend against human judgement receives the highest praise. And yet perhaps it is some merit, in some degree acceptable to God, if a person, whatever the intention, avoids in outward behaviour giving scandal to the Church, if the name of the Lord is not blasphemed among the infidels and if the Order to which one belongs is not dishonoured among the worldly-minded. And this, too, comes as a grace from God—to be inspired not only to do good, but to refrain from evil. Yet the latter is vain, if the former does not follow, as it is written: "Depart from evil and do good." And both are vain if not done for the love of God.

At every stage of my life (God knows this) up to the present time I have feared to offend you rather than God, sought to please you rather than him. Your orders and not any love of God made me put on the habit of religion. Reflect, then, what an unhappy life I must lead—one miserable beyond all others—if here I endure all this in vain, with no hope of reward in the future. For a long time my pretence deceived you as it did many others, so that you mistook hypocrisy for devotion. And so commending yourself to my prayers you ask of me what I look for from you.

Do not, I beg, hold me in such high esteem, for fear you cease to help me with your prayers. Do not think that all is well with me, lest you withdraw the grace of your healing. Do not think that I am not in need, lest you delay to succour me in my adversity. Do not believe that strength is mine, in case I fall for want of you to uphold me. False praise has brought injury upon many and it has taken from them the support of which they are in need. Through Isaiah the Lord cries: "O my people, they which lead thee cause thee to err and destroy the way of thy paths." And through Ezekiel he says: "Woe to the women that sew pillows to all armholes and make kerchiefs upon the head of every stature to hunt souls."[11] Whereas through Solomon it is said: "The words of the wise are as goads and as nails fastened by the masters of assemblies." That is to say, they do not know how to ease the wounds but to pierce them. Cease, I pray you, from your praise of me, else you will be found guilty on the base charge of flattery and falsehood. Or if you suspect there is good in me, the breath of my vanity may carry away the quality you have praised. No one having knowledge of medicine diagnoses an internal ailment from outward appearance. What is common alike to the reprobate and the elect wins no favour in the sight of God. Of such a kind are outward actions which are performed more zealously by hypocrites than by saints. "The heart is deceitful above all things and desperately wicked; who can know it?" And: "There is a way which seemeth right to a man, but the end thereof are the ways of death." It is rash to pass judgement in that which is reserved for the scrutiny of God. And so it is written: "Judge none blessed before his death." That is to say, do not praise a man when by praising him you can make him no longer praiseworthy.

And to me your praise is the more dangerous because I find pleasure in it. And the more anxious I am to please you, the more your praise takes me in and the more it delights me. Be fearful, I beg you, on my behalf always, instead of being confident in me, that I may be helped always by your solicitude. But now especially must you fear, when I no longer have in you a refuge from my passionate nature. I do not want you to exhort me to virtue or rouse me to the fight, saying: "For my strength is made perfect in weakness", and: "Yet is he not crowned, except he strive lawfully." I do not seek a crown of victory. It is enough for me to avoid danger. It is safer to avoid danger than to engage in war. In whatever corner of heaven God shall place me, he will do enough for me. There, none will envy another, since what each one will have, that will suffice. And that I may add to what I say the weight of authority, let us hear Saint Jerome: "I confess my weakness, I do not wish to fight in the hope of victory, lest thereafter I lose the victory." What need to abandon what is sure and follow the way of uncertainty?

CHAPTER VII

Talem, memini, subiecisti rationem.

[You showed, I remember, such good sense.]

Abelard writing to Héloïse
P.L. 1771.

WHAT were the feelings of Héloïse when she read Abelard's letter? Was she hurt by its coldness; then con-
soled by its warmth? Was she aggrieved at his desire to
dissociate himself from the past, then touched by the acknowledgement that he had loved her beyond measure? Was
she moved because to her, his wife, precisely because she was
his wife, he had entrusted his salvation? Her answer to these
questions, in so far as she has given one, is contained the four
words of the superscription that heads her reply. In it she
addresses in terms taken from logic the master who had instructed her in logic: *Domino specialiter, sua singulariter.*[12]
In species, *specialiter* (that is as a nun), she belongs to God;
as an individual, *singulariter*, she is Abelard's. Or as Charles
de Rémusat translates: *à Dieu par l'espèce, à lui comme in-
dividu.* She is a religious, but she has the distinction of being,
at the same time, the wife of Abelard. And not even to please
Abelard can she pretend that she believes herself—now any
more than when she took her vows—to have been given a
vocation to the religious life. Recognising, however, the note
of tension in Abelard's letter—the fact that he does not wish
to be reminded of the past and, with it, of his responsibility
for the present, she determines to do what she has always
done—act in the manner that she sees as being conducive to
his welfare. She can and must refrain from speaking of a mat-

ter on which it distresses him to have her speak. Therefore, that he may have no cause to blame her in anything (so she opens her letter), she has set his order as "a bridle" upon her lips, for though "the tongue speaks out of the fullness of the heart", *ex abundantia cordis os loquitur,* and when the heart aches it is hard for the tongue to be silent, nevertheless the hand of the writer can refrain from setting down the heart's longing. She need not give expression to her longing and henceforward she will not.

This could have meant an end to the correspondence. Instead, Héloïse found a theme on which it was not only permissible but desirable for the two to exchange ideas. As abbess of the Paraclete she asks its founder for instruction and guidance not for herself personally, but for the community; not for the immediate present only, but for the time to come. She makes a twofold request that Abelard should compose an exposition on the origins and purpose of the religious life for women; and secondly, a Rule to be observed at the abbey. In her previous letters Héloïse had stressed that at the Paraclete (in contrast to Saint-Gildas where his efforts were wasted) there was work awaiting him. She now presents him with a specific task for which, by reason of his scholarship, his experience in monastic houses, his position as founder of the Paraclete, he was pre-eminently suited. As for herself, she too will derive benefit—not only from the knowledge she will acquire, but because "as a new nail drives out an old so does a fresh train of thought expel from the mind the memory of things past".

The two previous letters of Héloïse were deeply personal. The third, after an opening that is no less so, is in the nature of a dissertation. And yet this letter, in its own way, reveals the personality of the writer. It shows her as scholarly, level-headed, independent, fearless, compassionate—an innovator rather than a traditionalist. It also throws light on the problems of the religious life as it was then lived. In asking Abelard to formulate a Rule she points out that in effect no such Rule exists for women. The one to which religious of either sex profess obedience was made by Saint Benedict for men. The very garments that the saint mentions are those of men. He speaks moreover of the abbot as receiving pilgrims and guests at table. Is an abbess to entertain men in this manner, share with them food and drink? Abelard must surely know how such gatherings can end. Saint Jerome warned his friends Paula and Eustochium. The pagan Ovid also bears witness. And here Héloïse quotes from the *Ars Amandi*—either from memory or from a copy at hand in the Paraclete:

> *Vinaque quum bibulas sparsere Cupidinis alas*
> *Permanet et coepto stat gravis ille loco . . .*
> *Tunc veniunt risus; tunc pauper cornua sumit;*
> *Tunc dolor et curae rugaque frontis abit . . .*
> *Illic saepe animos iuvenum rapuere puellae,*
> *Et Venus in venis, ignis in igne furit.*

[And when wine has sprinkled Cupid's thirsty wings, he stays; and the place he has occupied he resolutely holds. Then, laughter comes. Then, the poor man takes courage. Then, grief and care flee; and the wrinkled brow is smoothed. There often girls have snared the hearts of youths. Venus runs riot in the blood; and fire takes light from fire.]

Nor, she continues, if women alone were admitted would this be a solution. Women too can be corrupt; and a woman who is herself corrupt is quick to corrupt others. Besides, if men are to be excluded this must mean that persons who do the convent good service will take offence. And, apart from visitors, there are the deacons who are admitted to intone the Gospel in the night Offices. It is a matter of urgency that Abelard should lay down, once and for all, clear regulations "so that women leading lives consecrated to God may do so with greater sincerity and free from temptation".

As far as women are concerned, the entire Rule as now observed is at fault. Is it in all seriousness to be expected, Héloïse asks, that women should live in precisely the same manner as men? Are they to till the fields, bring in the harvest? It would be absurd to lay the same burden upon an ass as upon an elephant, to bring a bull and a heifer under the same yoke. Saint Gregory was aware that men and women should be treated differently: "Men are to be admonished in one way, women in another. Heavier burdens are to be laid on men, lighter on women." In his Rule for men Saint Benedict observed discretion regarding such matters as work, fasting, the drinking of wine. If he granted concessions to men, he would undoubtedly have done likewise had he made a Rule for women. Héloïse, her mind moulded by her classical reading, regards discretion as the mother of the virtues—and it is contrary to discretion that the two sexes should observe the same Rule. What precisely, then, is to be expected of women? This is a matter that requires to be clarified, if only because those who embrace the religious life should know what is involved. For what could be more absurd than to set out on a journey if there is no one to show the way? What more presumptuous than to choose and profess a manner of life of which next to nothing is known? Discretion, then, is the key—discretion coupled with reason. What does not accord with these cannot be regarded as good or virtuous, since the virtues themselves, if they pass beyond the bounds of reason, become, as Saint Jerome has said, vices. Moreover, those who bind themselves by a vow should not be strained to the last limit; they should be in a position to go, if they wish, beyond the letter of the vow—but this is impossible if the vow to begin with is too exacting.

The aim of the religious, as Héloïse sees it, should be, before all else, to live in accordance with the Beatitudes: in short, to aspire to be a Christian, not more than a Christian. To fulfil the teaching of the Gospels calls for a high degree of virtue. It means putting first things first. And this brings her to the consideration of what she calls *indifferentia*, things or practices which, being in themselves neither good nor bad, do not specifically prepare the soul for the kingdom of heaven or necessarily commend it to God. She is thinking, for example, of clothing, food, drink, fasting, abstinence. Here, again, discretion must dictate the norm. Although in theory Saint Benedict considered wine as not being for monks, he nevertheless permitted it as a concession to the times. Characteristic of her way of thought is her insistence that it is in abstinence from wrong-doing, not from food, that virtue consists, in as much as the kingdom of God is not in eating and drinking, but in "righteousness and peace and joy of the Holy Ghost".

Esteeming the spirit above the letter, she values intention before action and sees the virtues as existing primarily in the will. A person, she says, is virtuous in the will; that is, in the inner man, regardless of outward circumstances. She had said in her previous letter that chastity is a virtue of the mind. Reverting to this she enlarges upon it, quoting Saint Augustine: "Continence is a virtue not of the body but the soul. But the virtues of the soul are made manifest in the outer man, through his activities." She boldly maintains that continence was not unequal in John who did not marry and Abraham who begat sons and daughters. She quotes Saint Augustine on patience: "Patience was already in Job; the Lord knew this and gave testimony of it, but it was made known to men by the proof of temptation." It is, then, the virtue of the inner man that occupies her and it is virtue on this level, rather than outward practices of piety, that she would have stressed at the Paraclete. Virtue is the fruit of

prayer, in particular the liturgical prayer of the Church, which
is to be the centre of the religious life. But here again she
puts in a plea for discretion. If, for example, the psalter has
been recited in full before the completion of a week, must it
be obligatory, she asks, to begin to go through it for a second
time?

In all these matters Abelard is to be her guide. "To you
now, master, while you live, it falls to institute for us what
is to be observed here for all time. For you, after God, are the
founder of this place; you, through God, are the creator of
this congregation; you with God, shall be the establisher of
our way of life. After you, we shall, perhaps, have someone
else to instruct us, one who will build on another's foundation. He may, we fear, be less solicitous for us, and we ourselves less ready to hear; though he may be equally willing,
he may not be equally able. Speak to us, therefore, and we
shall hear."

Abelard did as Héloïse asked. He composed two treatises.
The first, which concerns the origins of the religious life for
women, is largely a eulogy of the feminine sex, in which he
dwells on the honour bestowed on women in the early
Church and, before that, in the Hebrew and the pagan
worlds. The second is a detailed Rule to be observed at the
Paraclete. The compiling of the Rule gave him particular
satisfaction. It was a task which he was confident of being
able to fulfil. Enthusiasm breaks through the ponderous and
sometimes crabbed writing. He is proud to declare his determination that, drawing partly upon tradition, partly upon the
testimony of the Scriptures and partly upon reason, he will,
by embodying these, "fashion out of many imperfect ele-
ments a perfect whole".

His Rule is perhaps in some respects more exacting than
Héloïse herself would have chosen. But in the main it follows
the lines she had suggested. Indeed, in part he hands back to

her, as it were, ideas that she had put to him, sometimes en-
larging upon these, sometimes transcribing passages word for
word from her letter. That her own ideas, even her words,
should be presented as his can only have pleased Héloïse.
She was ambitious not for herself, but for Abelard: she is
one of many women who down the centuries have been content that their ideas be given to the world not as their own,
but on the lips or in the writings of a lover, husband or friend.

Having dealt with the purpose and general principles of
the religious life, Abelard turns to the *minutiae* of the day-to-
day routine. Nothing is too small to command his attention.
The duties of the respective members of the community are
stated with precision. The wardrober, *vestaria*, is to see not
only that the wool is shorn from the sheep, the leather provided for making sandals—she must also allot to each individual her needle, thread, and scissors. With an old-maidish
exactitude he gives instruction as to the clothes of the nuns.
They must on no account go barefoot in the name of religion,
but wear stockings and shoes. Nor is the habit to be made in
an exaggerated style: it must not be so long as to trail on the
ground and pick up dust; nor should the sleeves fall below
the length of the arm and hand. He goes into the matter of
bed-clothes: each nun is to be allowed a mattress, a pillow,
a sheet, a blanket, and a bedspread.

As to food, except at times of fasting enjoined by the
Church, two meals a day are normal; though in winter—not
for reasons of mortification, but because the days are short—
one, he thinks, should be adequate. Meat may be eaten once
a day for three days of the week. On meatless days two vege-
table courses are to be provided. Spices are not permitted, and
bread is to be baked from coarse-grained flour. After a lengthy
discourse on wine—in particular the evils that can come of it—
he finally concedes that it may be taken provided it be mixed

with four parts of water. He quotes Aristotle as saying that women are less prone to drunkenness than are men.

Perhaps because he had himself known much physical suffering, Abelard is particularly concerned as to the care of the sick. Everything possible must be done for their bodily and spiritual welfare. Meat is not to be denied them; nor are they to be subject to the same rules as those who are in good health. There should be kept in mind the saying: *Infirmis non lex posita.* [The law was not made for the sick.] Medicines must be available, and the infirmarian should herself have knowledge of medical matters.

Abelard makes it clear that he would like there to be near the Paraclete a religious house for men, that the men may help the women and "a mutual affection" unite the two houses, the abbot in particular giving counsel to the abbess. Discussing this he at the same time lays down that access for men is to be rare and speech brief: *rara sit accessio, brevis locutio.* In fact, there was no such house in the vicinity of the Paraclete, possibly because Abelard saw at the beginning that his presence gave rise to gossip; nor could he have been expected to surrender to another his privileged position as director. There were, nevertheless, living within reach of the abbey, lay-brothers who undertook the cultivation of the land and helped in other tasks unsuited to women.

Taking up the point Héloïse had made concerning the entertainment of guests, Abelard discusses the duties of the portress. Someone of good sense must be allotted this task, who will know, when persons come knocking on the door, who should be admitted, who sent away. She must exclude men, except in special circumstances; and she must shut out gossip. Her manner should be pleasant. Let her recall the words: "A soft answer turneth away wrath", and be civil to those whom she lets in, and no less so to others who, for whatever reason, are sent away.

Weaving, spinning, baking; the care of bees, geese and hens
—these are some of the tasks allotted to the nuns. But adequate time is to be set apart for reading, studying, and the
illumination of manuscripts. All occupations, however, are
subordinate to the primary purpose of the religious life, the
recital of the Divine Office. Except for sickness no one may
absent herself from the eight canonical Hours or from daily
Mass. To enable the nuns to attend the night Offices without
detriment to health, enough sleep must be allowed. The
psalms that form part of the Hours are to be intoned dis-
tinctly, so that they can be understood; and chanting is to be
so modulated that it can be sustained by those whose voices
are not powerful. In the oratory everything must be done in a
fitting manner. No one is to read or sing what she has not
prepared—even so, no nun in practising her part, may do so
in a way that will disturb others who are sleeping. The oratory
is to be simple, its adornments necessary rather than superfluous, clean rather than costly. There are to be no statues—
and nothing made of gold or silver, except a silver chalice.
There shall be one pair of bells, and a vessel containing holy
water. On the altar is to stand a simple, wooden cross, on
which may be painted, if this be desired, a figure of the
Saviour.

A letter addressed by Abelard to the nuns of the Paraclete,
ad virgines Paraclitenses, bears witness to the importance that
he attached to study. Bidding them follow the example of
the women in whom Saint Jerome fostered a love of learning,
he urges that, as well as reading, they should learn languages.
Héloïse will instruct them, for they are indeed fortunate, he
tells them, in having for their mother one who is unique in
her day in being endowed with what the saint had looked
upon as a special grace—the knowledge of three languages:
Latin, Greek, and Hebrew.[13] This, Abelard continues, has

the advantage that, when in reading the Bible a difficulty of interpretation occurs, they will be able to think out a solution for themselves.

Much time was given to reading the Bible and to reflection on what was read. Héloïse wrote assuring Abelard that in this matter his wishes were being respected, in accordance with the injunction: *Ama scientiam Scripturarum et carnis vitia non amabis.* [Love the study of the Scriptures and you will hate the sins of the flesh.] Nevertheless, she goes on, sometimes the difficulties confronting the reader are such as to make the labour appear fruitless. And she reminds him how at Rome Marcella used to ply Saint Jerome with Biblical queries and was not content unless his answers satisfied her reason—so much so that at times the saint felt that he was in the presence less of a pupil than a critic. Inspired, then, by the example of Marcella, Héloïse and her sisters at the Paraclete venture to turn for help to Abelard. "As pupils approaching a master, daughters a father", they beg him to elucidate forty-two little questions, *questunculae*, set out in the order in which these have arisen in the course of reading.

Most of the questions (they came to be known as the *Problemata Heloisae*) arise out of the Gospels, others are suggested by passages in the Epistles or the Old Testament. Their tone reflects the independent mind of Héloïse. Some have a modern ring. She is not overawed by the inspired word of God, but boldly confronts her difficulties, not hesitating to question the sayings of Christ. What precisely is meant, she asks, by taking no thought for the morrow? Why should there be more joy in heaven over one sinner who has repented than over the ninety-nine who have done no wrong? What precisely is intended by the injunction to pray without ceasing? What justification has Christ for pronouncing a curse on the barren fig-tree—how could the tree be expected to bear fruit out of season? What, she wants to know, is the explanation

of conflicting accounts of the same incident—as, for example,
Peter's denial of his master? She is perplexed (as many have
been) by the differing versions of Christ's appearances after
the Resurrection: "The Evangelists," she says, "have left us
in the greatest confusion over the appearances of the risen
Lord to the women." Sometimes her difficulties belong less
to the sphere of Biblical studies than to that of moral theology—as when she considers the nature of sin, asking whether
it is possible to be guilty of sin in doing something that is
permitted or even commanded. Her brief, clear-cut queries
elicit from Abelard carefully thought out replies that sometimes extend into what amounts to a short treatise. As well
as these, Abelard wrote a commentary (called the *Hexameron*) on the six days of the Creation. This again was at a
request from Héloïse to clarify the account given in *Genesis*.
"You beg and implore me, implore and beg me", *supplicando
postulas et postulando supplicas*, he says in the preface.

Moreover it was to please her (*ad tuaram precum instan-
tiam* [at your urgent request], he writes in the accompanying
letter) that he composed a hundred and thirty hymns and
sequences for use at the Paraclete, many of which were well
known in the Middle Ages. At first he had demurred, excusing
himself on the ground that innovations were unnecessary,
indeed sacrilegious, when there were already in existence
numerous ancient hymns, some of which were attributed to
the saints. He suggested that the nuns should give reasons for
desiring a change. When they did so, he confessed that the
arguments put forward by Héloïse had won him over: *Talem,
memini, subiecisti rationem.* [You showed, I remember, such
good sense.] She had said (and, again, her objections have a
modern ring) that many of the hymns, even though they
might be written by Saint Ambrose or Saint Hilary or other
renowned composers, were so poor in rhythm that it was impossible to fit the words to music—besides which, many bore

no relation to the occasion for which they were appointed.
She further objected that, whereas for the rest of the Scriptures the version of Saint Jerome was in use, the translation
of the psalms was apocryphal.

Abelard sent the hymns in three lots, each accompanied by
a letter—the first addressed to Héloïse personally, the others
to the community. Some of the hymns are in honour of the
saints. The majority are for the Offices of the day and night;
or for the more important festivals of the Church throughout
the year, from the Nativity to the Resurrection and the As-
cension. Perhaps the best known is the hymn for Vespers on
Saturday evening, *Sabbato ad Vesperas*, beginning:

> *O quanta, qualia*
> *Sunt illa Sabbata,*
> *Quae semper celebrat*
> *Superna curia!*
> *Quae fessis requies,*
> *Quae merces fortibus,*
> *Cum erit omnia*
> *Deus in omnibus!*

In the disciplined Latin the words have a splendour and a
haunting nostalgia that are lost in the brassy English version
included in *Hymns Ancient and Modern*:

> "Oh, what the joy and the glory must be,
> Those endless Sabbaths the blessed ones see:
> Crown for the valiant, to weary ones rest;
> God shall be all and in all ever blest."

His simple verses for Candlemas evoke the scurry of feet
and the glimmer of tapers as young and old vie with one
another in their eagerness to honour the Virgin Mother
whose Son the aged Simeon shall proclaim as the Light to
lighten the Gentiles:

> *Beate senex, propera,*
> *Promissa comple gaudia,*
> *Et revelandum gentibus*
>   *Revela lumen omnibus.*

[Thou blessed at thy life's end, bring to swift fulfilment the joy promised us. Reveal to the world the Light for which all mankind is waiting.]

There is also a little elegant hymn for the Annunciation, that begins:

> *Mittit ad Virginem*
> *Non quemvis angelum,*
> *Sed fortitudinem*
> *Suam, archangelum,*
> *Amator hominis.*

[The Lover of mankind sends to the Virgin no ordinary angel, but an archangel, his own sovereign strength.]

Abelard composed thirty-four of what he calls "small sermons", *opuscula sermonum,* for the community at the Paraclete. These may have included some that he had preached when he was at the convent after establishing the nuns there. But the accompanying letter to Héloïse makes it clear that at least the majority were written at her request, and in some haste. It is a warm, relaxed letter, and shows Abelard's eagerness to carry out her wishes:

"After recently completing at your request a little book of hymns or sequences, Héloïse my sister whom I revere and love in Christ, I then, because you asked this of me, went on to compose in all haste and as best I could—for I am not used to this kind of writing—a number of small discourses for yourself and your spiritual daughters assembled in our oratory. Bearing in mind that these are to be read, not spoken, I have

tried to make my points in a straightforward manner, without
recourse to eloquence; to use words in their literal sense,
without rhetorical elaboration. Perhaps, indeed, a plain rather
than an ornate way of speech, in that it is more direct, will be
grasped more easily by simple minds. Moreover in view of the
kind of persons who will be listening, the very uncouthness of
everyday speech will in itself be an asset, giving to what I
have to say a pungency likely to commend it to the understanding of girls who are still young. In writing these, or
rather in arranging them, I have kept to the order of the
feasts of the Church, beginning with what was the beginning
of our Redemption.

"Farewell in the Lord, you who are his handmaid, once
dear to me in the world, now most dear to me in Christ:
then, in the flesh, my wife; now, in the spirit, my sister; and,
in following a way of life that is holy, my companion."

There is no longer the tension, so marked in Abelard's
early letters. A relationship that is acceptable to him has been
established between Héloïse and himself. At Saint-Gildas he
had reproached himself with having abandoned the oratory
which he founded. Now, he has the satisfaction of knowing that, raised to the status of an abbey, it is in the keeping
of Héloïse, who in her turn depends on him for guidance. His
labours have not been in vain. His vineyard is thriving. A
purpose, at a time when this was most needed, has been given
to his life; his spirit lifted, his vitality renewed. It is significant that the period during which Abelard, at the request of
Héloïse, was directing the affairs of the Paraclete, was for himself one of particular intellectual activity. He published his
Theologica Christiana; and two parts of his *Introductio ad
Theologicam*, begun probably as far back as 1114. He revised
the *Scito Te Ipsum* in which he examines the relationship
between the will and right or wrong action. The *Sic et Non* is

also thought to belong to this period, a treatise in which he sets out for appraisal conflicting texts from the Bible and the Fathers—not in a spirit of scepticism but on the principle that, through confronting difficulties, truth is attained. "By doubting," he says in the prologue, "we come to ask questions and by asking questions we perceive the truth."

That Abelard's philosophical and theological writings influenced the thought of Héloïse can hardly be in dispute. It is evident in her veneration of Saint Jerome; in her devotion to certain authors of classical Rome; in the importance that she ascribes to the intention behind an act, as distinct from the act itself; in her use of texts and quotations and in her imagery. But what of the reverse? Did Héloïse have any influence on Abelard's thought? Etienne Gilson in *La Théologie Mystique de Saint Bernard* suggests that she did, and that this influence (along with that of Cicero) is to be found in Abelard's teaching on the love of God as propounded first at the beginning of the *Introductio ad Theologiam* (condemned at Soissons in 1121) and developed at length in the *Expositio in Epistulam Pauli ad Romanos*, published about 1136. In the latter, commenting on the words from the *First Epistle to the Corinthians: Non quaerit quae sua sunt:* [(Love) seeketh not her own], Abelard says that perfect love of God means loving God solely for his own sake, independently of any advantage derived from this, even our eternal happiness. If we love God not for himself solely, but because of the happiness of heaven that we hope for from him, *pro regni felicitate quam ab eo speramus,* this, he says, does not deserve the name of love. Gilson, comparing Abelard's teaching with the concept of disinterested love as exemplified in the words and actions of Héloïse throughout her relations with Abelard, sees the first as a transposition into abstract terms of the second. Moreover, certain of Abelard's words in his commentary on *non quaerit quae sua sunt* echo those used by Héloïse in her sec-

ond letter in which she rejects as totally unworthy a woman
who seeks in her husband anything other than himself. As
though her words were fresh in his mind, Abelard writes that
a husband wants to be loved by his wife not for his riches but
for himself. "Since therefore," he continues, "you want your
wife to love you solely for your own sake [*gratis*], are you
going to love God for something other than himself?"

CHAPTER VIII

*N'en doutons pas, Pierre le Vénérable
connaissait admirablement Héloïse.*

Etienne Gilson, *Héloïse et Abélard.*

WHILE Abelard had remained in comparative obscurity
in Brittany his enemies had forgotten him or at least
lain low. When he was teaching again on the hill of Sainte-
Geneviève it was another matter. For as soon as his pupils
had once more gathered round him and his works became a
topic of discussion, he was noticed by William of Saint-Thierry
(a former enemy of his and a pupil of Bernard of Clairvaux),
who in his turn drew the attention of Bernard to what he
regarded as Abelard's dangerous teaching (*nova docet, nova
scribit*), especially that contained in his *Introductio ad Theologiam* and his *Theologica Christiana*, though he suspected
worse, he said, in the *Sic et Non* and the *Scito Te Ipsum*,
neither of which he had read. The outcome was that, after an
apparently amicable but fruitless meeting between Bernard
and Abelard, the former was instrumental in bringing about
the condemnation of Abelard in 1141 at the council of Sens,
held in the presence of Louis VII, the archbishop of Sens,
bishops, and lesser clerics. The condemnation was made in
Abelard's absence. For hardly had the assembly opened when,
moved by disgust, weariness, ill-health, or possibly the realisation that he was trapped, the accused threw in his hand: he
said that it was his intention to appeal to the sovereign authority of the Pope, and thereupon quitted the gathering.

It is not certain how far back in time the enmity between
Abelard and Bernard extends. Writing to Bernard after the

latter had paid a visit to the Paraclete, Abelard made it clear
that the abbot of Clairvaux had received a warm welcome:
Héloïse had said (when Abelard was at the convent afterwards on some business) that Bernard addressed the community "in the manner of an angel rather than of a man". It
is impossible to believe that she would have shown such enthusiasm, even if it were that of her sisters rather than her
own, had she thought of him as Abelard's enemy. Nevertheless,
in the same letter Abelard goes on in a tone that is now
ironic, now truculent, to rebut a criticism made by Bernard
to Héloïse at the time of the visit and passed on by her to
Abelard "on the quiet" (*secreto mihi intimavit*) concerning
the usage, in the recital of the Lord's Prayer at the Paraclete,
of the Vulgate version of Saint Matthew which runs *panem
nostrum supersubstantialem*[14] [our supersubstantial bread]
instead of the usual *panem nostrum quotidianum* [our daily
bread]. Moreover the tendency among scholars has been to
identify Bernard with one of the *novi apostoli* mentioned in
the *Historia Calamitatum* (Héloïse calls them *pseudo-apos-
toli*), who went up and down the country decrying Abelard's
teaching and his person so effectively that they brought him,
he says, into disrepute with the civil and ecclesiastical authorities and even with some of his friends, so that he began to
feel it would be preferable to live among the Saracens than
among Christians. There is also a letter that has come to
light in our own times, bearing the title *Contra Bernadum*,
in which Abelard, writing to adherents of his whom he addresses as *socii*, complains of one who having pretended to be
his friend turned out an enemy; who mocked his teaching,
calling his writing *stultilogiam magis quam theologiam* [the
study of folly rather than of God]: words which Bernard used
in a letter he later sent to Pope Innocent II, denouncing
Abelard.

Abelard and Bernard were both men of exceptional intel-

lectual powers. They were also overbearing, each as ready as
the other to impose his own views and clamp down on opin-
ions that did not meet with his approval. But whereas Abelard concerned himself primarily with personal triumphs won
over teachers or rivals in the field of dialectic, as well as with
a sincere attempt to present theology in terms acceptable to
reason, Bernard saw himself as the champion of orthodoxy,
called upon in the case of Abelard (and Abelard was not the
only such person) to do battle on behalf of the Church
against a dangerous innovator who was perverting the truth
and destroying the faith of the simple and God-fearing. Bernard had a colourful, dynamic personality that left its mark
upon his century more surely than did that of any of his
contemporaries. He is remembered and read today as is perhaps none of the others. He was highly-strung, deeply
emotional, prone to extremes, endowed with charm and not
without a sense of humour. He could display a disarming
gentleness that endeared him to his monks. Equally he could
be harsh and rigorous. Saint Francis de Sales says of Bernard
that until later in life when he came to realise his error he
used to frighten and discourage those whom he should have
helped. Moreover, Abelard brought out all that was worst in
him, for Bernard, despite his scholarship, had an almost path-
ological distrust of the intellectual approach to the understanding of religious truth. So extreme was he, so vehement,
a contemporary observed, that he was quick to view with
suspicion anyone who, in his opinion, was too attached to
secular studies. His hostility to Abelard is an instance. His
disapproval of Abelard's teaching takes the form not of dis-
passionate criticism, but of highly-coloured tempestuous
onslaughts in which, by reason of their vehemence and bitterness, he overstates his case. Writing to the Pope and the Roman Curia he calls Abelard a dragon that, having lurked
hitherto in its den, has now come into the open. Abelard is

presented as the persecutor of the Church, the enemy of Christ; one who casts before dogs what is holy; introduces profane novelties into doctrine; sets degrees and grades to the Trinity; offers poison concealed in honey. His pernicious ideas, Bernard thunders on, are bandied about at every cross-road. His books have wings that bear them from country to country, kingdom to kingdom. And it is not only his ideas that are at fault, it is the man himself. He is a monk without a Rule, a prelate without responsibilities, an abbot who argues with boys and consorts with women.

While Bernard stormed at the effrontery of Abelard in presuming to look for protection from the see of Peter, Abelard was on his way to Rome, confident that in the Holy City he would obtain a hearing. He was sixty years old (a more advanced age then than it is now), and the journey long and difficult. For hospitality, he went as was the custom, from monastery to monastery. But it was not at every religious house that Abelard the rebel, still less Abelard branded as a heretic, could hope to find a welcome. That he had set out at all is evidence of his courage. Formerly in his personal life he had played the coward, refusing in a desire for prestige to face the consequence of his actions. But in the intellectual sphere, in the pursuit of truth, he was fearless. So he continued on his way to Rome, only to learn (at what precise point in his journey we do not know) that his condemnation at Sens had been confirmed by the Pope.

Sens is hardly more than twenty-six miles from the Paraclete. Héloïse could not have failed to learn of the condemnation first by the council, then by the Pope. Abelard, for his part, knowing the pain this would cause her, the doubts it would awake were she to suppose that he, for whose sake she had embraced the religious life, were himself to be cut off from the Church; knowing, above all, the sympathy that would go out to him from Héloïse, addressed to her what is in part an *apologia* (one in which he honours the Church, but does not spare his enemies); in part a shout of triumph; by any estimate a declaration that only Abelard could have written. Héloïse is to have no fears, no anxiety. His persecutors may say what they please. They will not, and cannot, separate him from Christ:

"Héloïse my sister, once dear to me in the world and now most dear to me in Christ, logical thought has earned for me the hatred of men. The perverse, who pervert all that comes their way, for whom wisdom is nothing short of perdition, say that as a logician I am supreme, but that I am greatly in error in my interpretation of Saint Paul. They acknowledge my intellectual brilliance but question the purity of my faith as a Christian. In this respect, as I see it, they are as men who base their judgement on opinion rather than on the weight of evidence.

"I do not want to be a philosopher if I must reject Saint Paul. I do not want to be an Aristotle if he is to cut me off from Christ, 'for there is no other name under heaven whereby we must needs be saved'. I adore Christ who reigns at the right hand of the Father. I embrace him in the arms of faith, when in flesh born of a virgin by the power of the Holy Spirit, he makes manifest his glorious works. And so, to remove all anxiety, all restlessness and doubt from the heart within your breast, I want you to have my own words: I have established my conscience on the rock on which Christ founded his Church. I will give you my testimony in brief.

"I believe in the Father, the Son and the Holy Ghost: God who is one in nature; the true God in whom the Trinity of Persons does not contradict the unity of substance. I believe the Son to be equal to the Father in all things, in eternity, power, will, operation."

Having rejected as abhorrent to him the heresies of Arius and Sabellius and reaffirmed his belief in Christ's incarnation, passion, death and resurrection, and in consequence, his own resurrection ("I would call myself a Christian in vain if I did not believe that I would one day live again") he concludes: "This is the faith by which I live and in which my hope finds strength. Thus defended I do not fear the yelping of Scylla; I laugh at the whirlpool of Charybdis; I care nothing for the Siren's deadly songs. Though the tempest rage, I am not shaken. Though the winds blow, I am not moved. The rock of my foundation is sure."

As he journeyed on Abelard came to Cluny near Macon in Burgundy—to that most splendid of mediaeval abbeys; a religious house that was the mother of many such houses; renowned throughout Europe for its learning, its hospitality and, at this time, its magnanimous and cultured abbot, Peter the Venerable.

Pierre de Montboissier (his more usual appellation first appears in a letter of Saint Bernard) was born of noble parentage probably in the year 1093. He was the youngest of seven brothers, four of whom became clerics of high rank. His mother Raingarde, for whom he had a deep affection, took the veil (after she was left a widow) along with two granddaughters at the convent at Marcigny, a Cluniac foundation near Semur, which under her direction became famous as a centre of nursing and medical care. Professed at seventeen, he was a monk first at a monastery founded from Cluny at Vézelay and then at Fomène. From 1121 until his death in 1157 he was abbot of Cluny where at the beginning of his office he had to contend with hostility and dissension, a state

of affairs bequeathed him by his predecessors. In an age given
to extremes in thought and action, he was an advocate of discretion and tolerance. When faced with the criticisms levelled
against the Cluniac monks by Bernard he showed calm and
dignity. It was not a small matter to maintain friendly relations with the abbot of Clairvaux and at the same time pre-
serve his own integrity and independence. He achieved this
because he was calm, large-hearted and good-humoured; and
because he had the wisdom not to let differences of policy
and opinion concerning the practice of the religious life in-
trude upon what was a sincere friendship and one which grew
and deepened as the years went on.

His serenity of temperament (it was said of him that, like
his mother, he was always smiling) did not mean that he
lacked spirit. In defending his own Order against the attack
of Bernard he did not mince his words. When the abbot of
Clairvaux accused "his friends at Cluny" of deceit and rash-
ness, Peter asked by what right a "new breed of Pharisees"
thought fit to regard themselves as the only true monks
throughout the world. It was Bernard's manner and methods
that he took exception to. Peter knew of the abuses in his
Order, for he later accepted certain of Bernard's criticisms. In
a letter addressed to the Cluniac priors he inveighed against
religious who, wherever there was a smell of cooking, "gathered like hawks and vultures". On the other hand he was no
fanatic. Writing to a hermit he warns him of the dangers that
can arise from being too much alone. Solitude can breed
pride; lack of occupation develop into idleness; boredom en-
courage too much sleep; silence give way to gossip. An empty
mind, he says, resembles an empty house in which all manner
of fantasies find a lodging—the recluse pictures himself wearing a bishop's mitre and ruling over thousands of subordi-
nates; there is no position, however exalted, to which in his
dreams he does not aspire.

Apart from his services to his own abbey and its foundations, Peter the Venerable wrote theological works and verse.
He also wrote a quantity of letters in graceful, if rather flowery, prose, which, as well as throwing light on his personality,
are a commentary on the times. He travelled widely, though
in the course of his duties rather than for choice. He used to
dread having to go to Rome: the blazing Italian sun did not
agree with him and he disliked the food. While travelling in
Spain, he commissioned at Toledo a translation of the Koran.
Among those whom he chose for the task was an Englishman
named Robert Kennet. Peter the Venerable was a busy man.
He records how on one occasion the only time he could find
to read a letter from a friend was at the altar during the cere-
monies on Holy Saturday. Sometimes he used to take himself
off for a spell of peace to the neighbouring hills, from the
tops of which he could see in the distance the peaks of the
Italian Alps rising out of the clouds, and, spread far below,
the plain of France.

The abbey of Cluny was built (on the site of the original
church, founded in 910) under the direction of Saint Hugh of
Semur, at the juncture of the eleventh and twelfth centuries.
The high altar was consecrated in the year 1095. Reputed to
be the most splendid church in Christendom, it was certainly
the largest and continued to be so until Saint Peter's Rome,
was consecrated in 1626. Of it there remains today (since its
demolition at the beginning of the eighteen hundreds) little
else than the shell of part of the south transept, its massive
tawny stonework mounting in strong simple lines to be
crowned by a graceful octagonal belfry that dominates what is
still, to a large extent, a mediaeval town of Romanesque and
Gothic houses, zigzagging streets, towers, spires and clanging
bells. Something of the quality of the church's ornamentation, the vigour and simplicity of its carvings, can be seen
among the debris housed in what was once a granary and is

now the Musée du Farinier, close to the abbey. Adorning the broken capitals of pillars are figures, each one of them set in a shell-like medallion or merging into a pattern of foliage; each with an individuality of its own, its own character, its own life. A minstrel (a personification of one of the tones of the Gregorian chant) holds a zither, his head bent, the fingers of his right hand extended to twang the strings; a young man (one of the winds) energetically manipulates a pair of bellows: an abashed Adam and Eve stand under a tree laden with apples, a serpent coiled about the branches.

I saw Cluny in summer. The air had a resinous tang that came from the conifers growing close up to the abbey, their darkness accentuating the green of the grass and the silky blue of a sky in which clouds floated. Beyond the trees was the open country. At Cluny the country is never far away; it comes to view at a turn of a street or through an arched gateway—the river flashing silver as it winds over the cloud-swept emerald plain reaching away to the hills that Peter the Venerable knew, some of them undulating, their slopes planted with vines, others rising steeply to a summit shaggy with trees. It is a gracious countryside of wide horizons and small quiet towns that have musical names and Romanesque churches; Vézelay, Tournus, Anzy-le-Duc, La Bénissons-Dieu, Semur-en-Brionnais, Issy l'Evêque, Paray-le-Monial. The basilica at Paray-le-Monial was built more or less contemporaneously with Cluny. It is recorded in the life of Saint Hugh, abbot of Cluny, that while visiting Paray-le-Monial he healed a young monk who had been injured by a falling beam during the building of the choir. This must have been before 1109, the year in which Hugh died. Indeed, in some ways the church at Paray-le-Monial tells you more about Cluny as the abbey must have been in the twelfth century than do the ruins of Cluny itself. For the basilica is the abbey in miniature—not in every detail but in general appearance and atmosphere. It is a glori-

ous church, standing at a cross-road for all the world to see.
A row of little trees grow in front of it, and tall trees make a
backcloth of green. It deserves a long look. Look at the porch
on the west front. Sturdy pillars (each consists of four blocked
into one) support the weight of the low, deep-arched roof,
their capitals ornamented with foliage and the strange, staring
faces of beasts. Look at this porch by day when its stone is
golden. And again at night, when the shadows creep under it,
crowding for shelter below the arches; when the little trees
whisper to one another in the wind and the sky is dusted with
stars. Look at the basilica from the east, under a flushed morning sky. It mounts stage by stage, its massive golden stone
roofed with mellow red-brown tiles. On the ground-level
chapels fan out. Above these is the ambulatory; then the apse;
then the chancel—directing the eyes gradually to the octagonal belfry that dominates the solid harmonious whole. The
strength and simplicity of the outside have their counterpart
in an interior beautiful in its proportions and devoid of superfluous ornamentation. Its splendour is one that transcends
time. When a preacher mentioned Peter the Venerable, he
might have been speaking not of a figure out of history, but of
a well-loved neighbour.

Abelard was blessed in finding welcome at Cluny with a
man devoid of envy and generous of soul,

> *nescius invidiae, vena fuit veniae;*

one who was able to appreciate another's intellectual qualities, and be tolerant. Nor was the welcome a conventional
gesture of charity. Peter the Venerable, knowing that Abelard had reached the limit of his endurance, determined that
the wanderer would find at Cluny not a temporary resting
place, but one from which he could not be driven away. Having first of all brought about—with what degree of tact and

patient persuasion we cannot know—a reconciliation between Abelard and Bernard, he wrote to Pope Innocent II a letter that is a model of discretion. Having assured the Pope that Abelard, to whom the thought of heresy is "abhorrent", has been reconciled with Bernard and has consented to curb his language and remove from his writings anything likely to give offence, he goes on to beg on behalf of himself and his monks that Abelard, who has decided to give up the schools, may in view of his age and religious profession be authorised to remain permanently at Cluny where his learning, "with which his Holiness is well acquainted may be of benefit to all". "Deign to grant", he concludes, "that he may spend the last days of his life, which are perhaps not many, in your abbey of Cluny. Grant that nothing be permitted to disturb or drive away the sparrow from its place under the eaves, the dove from its nest. By the kindness you show all good men and the love you have bestowed on him too (*etiam istum dilexistis*) grant that he be defended by the shield of your apostolic protection."

Formerly wherever Abelard had taken himself, he brought with him trouble and turbulence. At Cluny all was peace. He had found the tranquillity for which his restless spirit had craved and the lack of which had accentuated the less pleasing traits in his personality. Fear of spiteful tongues had denied him at the Paraclete the haven which could have been his. Here was a haven of another kind, but serving a like purpose; a place where he knew that he was welcome, one where undisturbed he could follow his natural bent. Whether he taught, in the strict sense of the word, is not known. The fact that he is mentioned as walking in procession immediately in front of Peter the Venerable may mean that he was master of the oblates' school—the *consuetudines* of the Order laid down that at major feasts the master and pupils should take their place in front of the abbot. In any case he occupied himself, as Peter the Venerable wrote later to Héloïse, "with the things of the mind"—reading, prayer and meditation. He was quiet in demeanour, abstemious in food, simple in dress —Peter the Venerable, walking behind him in procession, used to notice Abelard's shabby, worn habit: "Saint Germain was not more humble; nor Saint Martin more divested of earthly riches". He spoke little—only when courtesy required him to take part in a conversation with his brethren or when, in theological discussion, he was pressed for an opinion. He offered the sacrifice of the Mass as often as was permitted, and every day after he had been restored to favour with the Holy See.

When Abelard's health began to deteriorate, Peter the Venerable, concerned for his welfare, sent him to a Cluniac foundation at Saint-Marcel near Chalon-sur-Saône, choosing this place because the climate was the mildest in that part of Burgundy and the monastery pleasantly situated—being near the town, yet the river flowing between: *prope urbem sed tamen Arari interfluente*. Here Abelard continued his studies, devoting himself to his books: "There was scarcely a moment when he was not either praying or reading or writing". Death did not find him asleep but ready waiting, "his lamp filled with oil—that is to say, his conscience at rest". He made his profession of faith, confessed his sins, received the sacrament of Christ's Body—"to all of which", Peter the Venerable concludes, "the monks of Saint-Marcel bear witness". He died on April 21, 1142, aged sixty-two, and was buried in the monastery church where his body remained until November, when Peter the Venerable took it to the Paraclete.

The following lines are thought to have been written by Peter the Venerable:

Gallorum Socrates, Plato maximus Hesperiarum
Noster Aristotles, logicis quicumque fuerunt
Aut par, aut melior; studiorum cognitus orbi

Princeps; ingenio varius, subtilis et acer;
Omnia vi superans rationis, et arte loquendi
Abaelardus erat; sed tunc magis omnia vicit,
Quum Cluniacensem monachum moremque professus,
Ad Christi veram transivit philosophiam
In qua longaevae bene complens ultima vitae,
Philosophis quandoque bonis se connumerandum
Spem dedit, undenas Maio revocante Kalendas.

[Socrates of the Gauls, mighty Plato of the West, our Aristotle, the equal of all philosophers that have been, or greater; acknowledged throughout the world as a prince in scholarship; versatile in genius, subtle and keen of wit; victorious in every conflict by force of reason and the gift of eloquence —such was Abelard. But he won his greatest victory when, professed a monk at Cluny, he left all for the true philosophy of Christ; on the twenty-first day of April, he brought a long life to a fitting close, leaving behind the hope that hereafter he be counted among philosophers of true worth.]

I came to Saint-Marcel on an evening in September. There was a sharpness on the air, and the sky was a pale, washed blue flaked with tiny clouds, like the scraps of wool that sheep leave behind on brambles and hedgerows. The hands of the church clock pointed to half-past six. It was a plain, flat-faced church Romanesque in style; the tall square belfry roofed rather steeply with slate. To the north-west was a lime-tree, its foliage touched with the first shrivelled brown of autumn. The west door, under a rounded arch surmounted by a triangular pediment, was closed. I knocked at an entrance to the nearby convent of Les Sœurs de Saint-Joseph de Cluny, which occupies the site of what in Abelard's day had been the monastery. I must have approached from the back, for I was taken through a flagged kitchen along a passage into a parlour. A nun came in. She was small and her movements neat and quick. We went through the garden, past a walnut-tree and along a path bordered with dahlias and pansies. She took out a bunch of large keys and going ahead of me unlocked a door in a wall, and then another. We went up and down stone steps through darkness, the nun reaching out her hand to guide me, until we came into a large rather bleak church. I noticed in the half-light a statue of Saint Isidore standing beside a yoke of oxen. This church, the greater part of which goes back to the eleven hundreds, is on the site of one built in the sixth century in honour of Saint Marcel who was put to death under the emperor Marcus Aurelius. A hole in the floor purports to be the opening of the well into which the saint's body was flung. Near this, on the south wall, is an inscription to the effect that the body of Abelard "a Frenchman and monk of Cluny"[15] was buried here before being removed to the Paraclete. The niche where the body rested was at that time part of the chapel of Notre-Dame which adjoined the cloister: after the Revolution chapel and cloister were demolished. In this chapel and then in the church (when the chapel had been destroyed) was a sarcophagus, on the lid of which was carved the recumbent figure of a monk wearing the Benedictine habit. This was either the coffin in which Abelard's body had originally been placed; or else a cenotaph raised in his memory by the monks of Saint-Marcel. In any case it is the sarcophagus in which the bones of Héloïse and Abelard now rest in the cemetery of Père-Lachaise. In the eighteen hundreds the artist Alexandre Lenoir had the head of the monk replaced by one made from a cast of Abelard's skull. He had a corresponding effigy made to represent Héloïse.

We went out of the church, the nun and myself, into the garden. The sun was low now, the sky a sheet of liquid gold. A muffled roar of passing cars came from the road. But it was quiet in the garden. A bird twittered. A walnut thudded to

the ground. There was a smell of burning leaves. I looked back
at the church. There are places, I thought, to which one returns or thinks to return; others to which a return is unlikely.
I had come here for a specific purpose, to follow Abelard's
story, in so far as it impinged on that of Héloïse, to the end.
It was improbable that I would come again. I wanted to hold
this moment in the garden at Saint-Marcel, in the shadow of
the Romanesque church, under the golden sky—but already,
faster than my thoughts, it was slipping from me.

We went back into the convent, through a room in which
there were old people sitting at a table, drinking soup from
bowls. The nun smiled at them and waved. Some smiled in
return and bowed; others had the withdrawn look one sees at
times on the faces of the very old, as though they were carved
in stone. The nun came out with me on to the road: she had a
friend who would drive me back to Chalon-sur-Saône. We
passed cottages with flower-gardens in front. Children ran up
seizing the nun's hand and chattering. Presently I was in a
car—a young man at the wheel, and in the back laughing
children. I waved to the nun and she to me. As the car crossed
the Saône the gold of the setting sun flashed on the darken-
ing water.

The letter in which Peter the Venerable tells Héloïse about
Abelard's last days at Saint-Marcel is remarkable not only for
the picture it gives of Abelard, but because it shows in what
esteem Héloïse was held by the abbot of Cluny. And it was
not simply esteem—Peter the Venerable understood her:
Pierre la connaissait bien. When he stressed the fact that
Abelard had ended his life among those who had shown appreciation of his greatness, he knew that this knowledge more
than anything would help to lighten her sorrow. He also knew
that it was a time to appeal to all that was finest in her personality: her steadfastness, her fidelity, her courage, her intel-

lectual qualities; that in stressing these he would help her to
live in a manner worthy of herself.

After thanking Héloïse for a letter he had received from
her (this is not extant) he tells her that he would have written sooner had he not been beset with demands on his time.
He had wanted to do so. And besides he had not yet thanked
her for gifts she had sent. His tone is warm, that of a friend
writing to a friend whom he reveres. "My affection," he says,
"does not begin now. It goes back a long way. I was hardly
more than a boy—scarcely a young man—when the fame not
yet of your religious life, but of your noble and admirable
studies came to my knowledge." People were talking of this
wonder, a woman still living in the world, yet devoting herself
to the pursuit of literature and philosophy, allowing nothing
—not the pleasures of the world nor its attractions nor its
delights—to deter her from the praiseworthy ambition to
study the liberal arts. She had stood out not only from those
who were indifferent to learning (always the majority, however intellectual an age may be); even among those who
cared, she was pre-eminent. "You surpassed," he writes,
"all women and nearly all men": *et mulieres omnes et pene
viros universos superasti.*

Then her life took a new direction, when entering the cloister she exchanged "logic for the Gospels, physics for Saint
Paul, Plato for Christ". Knowing the magnitude of the sacrifice she had made, Peter the Venerable is determined that
she will not see this sacrifice as wasted. In religion no less
than in the world she has been triumphant. She is the woman
of supreme courage, as brave as Queen Penthesilea, as reso-
lute as the prophetess Deborah. She is a fiery coal. She is a
lamp that shines to give light to others. He is telling her this,
he assures her, not to flatter but to give her heart (*non adu-
lando, sed exhortando*) that she may persevere in accordance
with the grace that has been bestowed on her. He would have

liked to talk on such matters at greater length, so impressed is he by her reputation for erudition and by all he has heard about her life as a religious. His sole regret is that she does not belong to Cluny. He would have liked to think of her as a nun at the convent of Marcigny (where his mother had entered), for excellent though this convent is, her presence would have enriched it. Yet if Cluny may not have Héloïse, it has had Abelard—"Your Abelard whose name must always be held in esteem, the servant and true philosopher of Christ, whom in the last years of his life Providence brought to Cluny, thus enriching it with a gift more precious than gold or topaz." "Your Abelard." Peter the Venerable had been silent as to the circumstances that brought Héloïse into the cloister. Yet in these two words he acknowledges all. He does not pretend that what has been has not been. Equally he does not fall back on platitudes. He sees Providence at work in things as they are, not as they ought to be or might have been. He relates the past to the present, in a passage that rings out with a glorious optimism reminiscent of Julian of Norwich.

> All shall be well
> And all manner of thing shall be well.

Héloïse is not to mourn Abelard as lost to her. They belong to each other both by the law of the flesh and the law of the spirit. Because they belonged in time, so they belong in an eternity that is here and now and for ever: "My revered and most dear sister in Christ, he to whom you were united first in the flesh and then in the stronger and more perfect bond of divine charity, with whom and under whom you long served the Lord, now rests in the bosom of Christ. Christ cherishes him in your place, indeed as a second you (*loco tui, vel ut te alteram in gremio suo confovet*), and he will restore him to you of his grace on the day that the Lord shall come down from heaven at the voice of the archangel and the sounding of the trumpet."

Abelard, when in peril of his life at Saint-Gildas, had asked that after his death his body should be brought to rest at the Paraclete. His words had unnerved Héloïse; the thought of his death had been unbearable to her. But when the time had come she was able, through the help of Peter the Venerable, to carry out his wishes. On the pretext of making a visitation, the abbot of Cluny went to Saint-Marcel early in the November that followed Abelard's death; and one night, while the monks slept, he had the body disentombed and taking it with him immediately set out for the Paraclete. He reached his destination on the sixteenth of the month, gave the body into the care of Héloïse, said Mass in the presence of the community and preached.

Abelard had died a monk of Cluny. It was therefore the privilege of the Order to have his body in their possession. But Peter the Venerable, for the sake of Héloïse, had surrendered this privilege to the abbey of the Paraclete; and he had done so (as is shown by the secrecy that he observed), at no little trouble to himself.

Héloïse was deeply moved. Writing to the abbot of Cluny, after he had left the Paraclete, she is at a loss to convey her gratitude for his visit but most of all for having brought "the body of the master". Unable to formulate her thoughts—then unable to find words in which to express them, she turns to practical matters. During his visit Peter the Venerable had promised that a *tricenarium* of Masses (that is a Mass to be said every day for thirty days) should be offered on her behalf at Cluny after her death. She asks him to confirm this in writing—thus showing her good sense, since in the event of a change of abbot, the Masses, if there were no record, might not be said. She also asks for a sealed letter confirming that

Abelard's body has been made over to her, and an assurance
that, before he died, he had received absolution for his sins.
Again she is wise in forestalling any attempt that might be
made to reclaim Abelard's body. The absolution, which was
to be hung, as was customary, above the tomb, was important as evidence that Abelard, should anyone want to brand
him as a heretic, had died loyal to the Church. Finally, she
makes a plea on behalf of her son Astralabe, a young man of
about twenty-four, that Peter the Venerable should use his
influence to obtain for him a prebend.

The letter is clear, concise, and warm:

"The mercy of God came down upon us in the grace of a
visit from your Reverence. We are filled with joy and pride,
my dearest father, because despite your exalted position you
have condescended to the level of our lowliness. For a visit
from you is something of which even persons of importance
are proud. Others are fully aware of the benefits conferred on
them by the presence of your Reverence. For my own part I
cannot formulate my thoughts, still less put into words the
blessing and comfort your visit has been to me. You, our lord
abbot, on the sixteenth day of November last, celebrated here
a Mass in which you commended us to the Holy Spirit; you
nourished us in chapter with the word of God; you made over
to us the body of our master, thus surrendering to us a privilege that belonged to Cluny. Moreover to me—whom though
unworthy to be named your servant, you in your gracious
humility have not disdained, in writing and in speech, to address as sister—you showed a particular mark of your sincere
affection in granting a *tricenarium* of Masses to be said on
my behalf at the abbey of Cluny after my death. You said,
too, that you would confirm this gift with your seal. It is this
promise made to your sister or, I should say, your servant,
that I now beg you my brother or rather my lord, to make

good. Also of your kindness be pleased to send me under your seal a document containing in clear terms the absolution of our master, to hang above his tomb. Remember, too, for the love of God, our Astralabe and yours, that you may obtain for him some prebend from the bishop of Paris or in some other diocese. Farewell. And may the Lord keep you and grant us from time to time the happiness of your presence."

Peter the Venerable's reply reflects his pleasure at the enthusiasm Héloïse had shown regarding his visit. He makes it clear that for his part it had been no duty-visit. He had felt at the Paraclete that he was welcomed not as a traveller or pilgrim, but as though he belonged to the household. And now that he has gone he feels that he still belongs. The kindness that he was shown was, he says, a mark of real charity, real warmth; and he wants to repay it as best he can. He gladly confirms the *tricenarium* of Masses. Also he sends the absolution signed and sealed:

Ego Petrus, Cluniacensis abbas, qui Petrum Abaelardum in monachum Cluniacensem suscepi, et corpus eius furtim delatum Heloisae abbatissae et monialibus Paracleti concessi, auctoritate omnipotentis Dei et omnium sanctorum absolvo eum pro officio ab omnibus peccatis.

[I Peter abbot of Cluny, who received Peter Abelard as a monk into the Order of Cluny and having secretly removed his body gave it over to the abbess and nuns of the Paraclete, on the authority of Almighty God and all the saints absolve him by virtue of my office from all his sins.]

As to Astralabe, Peter the Venerable is again anxious to help, but he has to admit that bishops can be difficult: "On behalf of your Astralabe, and because yours mine, I shall do my best to see that he is given a prebend in some church of distinction. It is not, however, an easy matter. I have often found bishops tiresome when it comes to granting prebends; they put all kinds of obstacles in the way. Even so, for your sake I shall do what I can as soon as I can."

The son of a famous father rarely enjoys a comparable fame. Telemachus is known less in his own right than as the son of Odysseus. He, however, as Homer has presented him, was a self-assured, level-headed young man who enjoyed his father's renown. There are other sons less happy, who, measuring themselves against a father's attainment, feel inadequate and so lose heart. The young Marcus Cicero was one of these. Others, again, are no more than names drifting upon the stream of time, their sole claim to be remembered resting upon a father's renown. Such was Astralabe. Apart from his personality of which we know nothing, the facts concerning him are few. We know that his mother looked forward with joy to his birth; that in obedience to her lover she travelled from Paris to Brittany where the child was born. It was she who gave him his name. *Astralabium nominavit.* [She named him Astralabe.] What does the name signify? Some have wanted it to mean a bright star, but etymologically there appears to be no justification for this. The word could suggest a star making its path across the sky, or perhaps a shooting star. The Latin root LAB- or LAP- is found in words that denote the movement of the heavenly bodies. Virgil writes:

> *Saepe etiam stellas vento impendente videbis*
> *praecipites caelo labi.*

[Often too when the wind is on the way you will see shooting stars pass across the night sky.]

And again:

> *medio volvuntur sidera lapsu*

[The stars turn in midst of their gliding course.]

Héloïse and Abelard were familiar with Virgil. On the other hand the word *astrolabium* (the name of Abelard's son is sometimes given as Astrolabius) was applied in the Middle Ages to a flat spherical instrument, used in the system of Ptolemy for measuring the heavens. Chaucer wrote a *Treatise on the Astrolabe* for his ten-year-old son Lewis. Possibly the word had a private association for Héloïse and Abelard. However that may be, soon after the child's birth (it may have been no more than a couple of months) his mother set out from Brittany to Paris, leaving her son in the care of Abelard's sister. Of Astralabe's upbringing nothing is known. Dearth of information has given rise to fantasy: George Moore pictures him as visiting his mother when she was in the convent at Argenteuil and later taking part (this is a chronological impossibility) in the children's crusade.

If Astralabe has little place in the story of Héloïse and Abelard, it does not mean that his parents were indifferent to him—the joy felt by Héloïse in anticipation of his birth belies this, as does the urgency of her plea to Peter the Venerable: "Remember for the love of God our Astralabe and yours": *Memineritis et amore Dei nostri Astralabii et vestri.* She has no need to go into explanations. Peter the Venerable clearly knows the circumstances. Her words suggest also that he knows Astralabe. Was Astralabe either then or earlier at Cluny? Was he there at the same time as his father? As to Abelard, the fact that he saw to it that his son was born in the home of his own sister speaks for itself. There is moreover a note of pathos in his telling of how, when he and Héloïse returned from Brittany to Paris for the marriage, they left behind their little son. Often men of intellectual brilliance like to think that they will pass on their gifts to a son. Perhaps Abelard was one of these. He wrote some forty verses, *Monita ad Astralabium*, addressed to his son (now on the threshold of manhood), "the joy of his father's life":

Astralabi fili, vitae dulcedo paternae.

The poem ranges over a wide field of subjects that include the value of study, the avoidance of evil-doing, the advantage of the written as distinct from the spoken word. There is mention of "a frequent complaint" made by Héloïse, *Eloysae crebra querela*, that if her salvation depends on her forgetting the joys she had known with Abelard, there can be little hope for her.

It is not known whether Astralabe obtained the prebend. A cartulary of the church of Buzé in Brittany records that in the year 1150 there was a canon of the cathedral of Nantes called Porcarius and that he had a nephew whose name was Astralabe. This Astralabe could be Abelard's son and Porcarius the brother whom he mentions having visited at Nantes. An Astralabe is mentioned in the necrology of the Cistercian Abbey of Haute-Rive in the Swiss canton of Freiburg. And there was a sub-prior at Argenteuil in 1152 (after the convent had been taken over by Saint-Denis) called Guillaume Abaelar, believed by some to be Abelard's son under another name. Finally, in the necrology of the Paraclete, the death of Abelard's son is recorded in an entry of October 30th, in which his father's name is added to his own: *Petrus Astralabius magistri nostri Petri filius.* [Peter Astralabe the son of Peter our master.]

CHAPTER IX

Ipsum oratorium cum omnibus ei pertinentibus concessi et donavi.

[I made over to them (i.e. Héloïse and her nuns) as a gift the oratory itself and all the property connected with it.]

Abelard. *Hist. Calam.* P.L. 169

"I want to know whether the Paraclete yu pass'd by is the same where the convent stands which was found'd by Abelard & wh. is so well known here, by Mr Popes Letter from *Eloisa.*"

Lady Hertford writing to her son in 1743

SO closely related are the lives of Héloïse and Abelard that in a sense her story comes to an end with Abelard's death and the bringing of his body to the Paraclete. Her last letter is the one in which she asks Peter the Venerable for the absolution to hang above her husband's grave; and the last addressed to her is Peter the Venerable's reply.

She lived on after her husband's death for just over twenty-two years, until May 16th, 1164, during which time, according to the chroniclers of her own and the following century, she kept faith with Abelard, offering constant prayers on his behalf: *Magnum ei post mortem in assiduis precibus fidem conservavit.* But Héloïse was not only the widow of Abelard, she was the abbess of what had become an important religious house. In the dry documents concerned with the Paraclete, her name shines like a star through the darkness of the centuries. It appears with expressions of affection and respect in the papal bulls that come in hot haste one upon another—those of Lucius II, Eugenius III, Anastasius IV, Adrian IV (the Englishman, Nicholas Breakspear), and Alexander III; each ratifying the privileges, with additions where these occurred, granted by Innocent II in 1131 and confirmed in 1136, when he stipulated that neither at the election of an abbess nor on any pretext whatsoever was the bishop or anyone else to presume to disturb or annoy the nuns: *ne nullum gravamen vel molestiam inferre praesumat*. It appears again in the charter of King Louis VII, in which he confirms the privileges granted by his father Louis VI, to the effect that the nuns of the Paraclete and those serving them should be immune from the payment of duty on anything throughout the kingdom bought or sold for the needs of the community.

At first Héloïse and her nuns had suffered privation. Then, as things improved and neighbours offered to help—factors which Abelard attributes to the working of the Holy Spirit, but also to the excellence of Héloïse as superior—the holdings of the convent gradually increased. A list of these, with the names of donors, contained in the bull of Pope Eugenius in 1147 (four years after Abelard's death) includes fields, meadow-lands, woods, vineyards, fishponds, mills, farm-buildings. Candles are mentioned as having been given for the feast of the Purification; and, presented by Margaret viscountess de Marrolis, a measure of wheat and twenty hens. Moreover, an archdeacon of Châlons, uneasy about money unlawfully acquired by his forebears, made over the amount "to the poor nuns of the Paraclete". Gifts were made by a certain Galo whose sister-in-law took the veil; and tithes paid by Raoul Jaiacus and his wife Elisabeth "for charity's sake and on account of a niece who became a nun". With improved circumstances the Paraclete was in a position to buy what was needed. Héloïse is mentioned as having bought tithes from Milo, a native of Nogent-sur-Seine.

On the spiritual level the reputation of the Paraclete was high. What Pope Adrian calls the "fragrance of its spiritual-

ity" attracted postulants, among whom were two nieces of
Abelard, Agathe and Agnès: Agnès became prioress in suc-
cession to a certain Astrane, the first to hold that office. As
time went on it became necessary to found daughter-houses.
In the course of some twenty years (between 1142 and 1163)
Héloïse established six such houses, listed as belonging to the
Ordo Paraclitensis. These were the abbey of La Pommeraie
and the priories of Sainte-Madeleine-de-Traînel, Laval, Noë-
fort, Saint-Flavit, and Saint-Martin-de-Boran which was also
known as Saint-Martin-aux-Nonnettes. Sainte-Madeleine-de-
Traînel, according to a bull of Innocent II, was to the west
of the Paraclete, on the river Orvin: the building with all
that belonged to it had been made over to the abbey by a
priest named Gundric, who owned the land on which it stood.
Its foundation is described in a charter drawn up by Hugo,
archbishop of Sens, whose role it was to hand over the keys
to "the lady Héloïse", and to charge Anselm of Traînel, over-
lord of the property and benefactor of the Paraclete, to care
for these "servants of Christ" and provide for their needs,
"for love of God and for the health of his soul". The archbishop also approved gifts already made by Anselm, as well as
others that he intended to make. Finally, having welcomed
the nuns with the greatest respect before the assembled company, he introduced them "to this place in which henceforth
they were to love and serve God". This priory was the scene,
probably in 1133, of a reconciliation between Héloïse and the
abbot of Vauluisant after a disagreement about an oak-wood.
Finally the wood was ceded to the Paraclete, on condition
that pigs belonging to the convent should not feed there,
since the abbot had established his right to the acorns.

The archbishop of Sens drew up two documents concerned
with the abbey of La Pommeraie. The first, which belongs
between 1144 and 1147, established that the land on which
the convent was afterwards built had been given to the Para-

clete by Baudouin de Closfontaine, with the consent of his
sons and his wife Anne (from whom he had received it), on
condition that each year, on the Nativity of John the Baptist,
the Paraclete should pay him a fixed sum. In the second, the
archbishop says that Héloïse had made over "the place known
as La Pommeraie" to Mathilde, countess of Blois, wife of
Thibaud, for her to build an abbey. In return, the countess
promised, with the consent of her sons, to give to the Paraclete annually three hogshead of wheat from the mill at
Provins-sous-Crèvecœur. The first abbess of La Pommeraie
was canonically elected from the "ladies of the Paraclete".
Future abbesses were to be elected from the community itself. Should this not be possible, the nuns of La Pommeraie
were to go to the Paraclete and choose an abbess from there:
they were not to appoint an abbess from a convent following
a Rule other than that of the Paraclete. Moreover, once a
year the abbess of La Pommeraie was to visit the Paraclete to
be instructed in the Rule. Likewise the abbess of the Paraclete
was to go to La Pommeraie and at a meeting of the chapter
amend the Rule, should this be necessary, and discuss points
arising out of it. These conditions, binding on both convents,
were not to be changed—not by the Pope himself—unless
with the consent of both parties.

The Paraclete is in Champagne in the department of Aube,
some fifty miles to the east of Paris, in the direction of
Troyes. It is five miles from Nogent-sur-Seine, between the
villages of Saint-Aubin and Quincey. These facts I had learnt
from books. Yet even so I found it hard to visualise the abbey
as having any kind of existence in our own day, so closely
was it linked in my thoughts with persons and events of over
eight hundred years ago. My pleasure, therefore, was all the
greater as I travelled by an early morning train one day in
August 1963 to visit, by courtesy of the owner, the Château

of the Paraclete, which, built in 1685 within a few minutes'
walk of the site on the bank of the Arduzon where had stood
Abelard's original oratory, had remained until 1793 the residence of the lady abbess.

As Paris was left farther and farther behind I had an increasing sense of unreality, of being drawn into a dream-like
world of the past. It was partly the rhythm of the train, lulling
me into a mood of reverie. It was also the landscape. Open
country broken now and again by low flat-topped hills
stretched away under a wide sky to far horizons. Clouds flung
their shadows on cornfields ripe for the harvest and on pas-
tures where horses and black and white cattle grazed. Here
and there, standing up in isolation, was a clump of evergreens,
their mysterious darkness bringing to mind the ancient, sacri-
ficial groves of pre-Christian Gaul. The colours of the landscape were delicate. The blue hills, the bronzed corn, the
faded gold of haystacks, pinkish-cream farmsteads—all were
muted by the bleached pallor of a chalk soil. And as often in
a landscape of chalk there was a compelling sense of a primae-
val past. I was reminded of the English countryside round
Salisbury. There was the same clear light, the space and the
silence—a silence that I could feel above and beyond the
rhythm of the train. Later, trees closed in on either side of
the railway-track, their nearness intensifying the sound of the
train, yet not so as to eliminate the silence. Looking out I
could see trees reaching ahead, making a tunnel of green;
and then, as the track curved, steel lines glinting.

The château is a pleasing harmony of mellow brick and
pearl-grey stone, approached by low wide steps and set about
by trees, lawns, and flower-beds. It has all the dignity proper
to the *Grand Siècle* tradition. A double row of nine tall windows, their woodwork painted white, and above these a rather
steeply pitched roof surmounted by tall chimney stacks, con-
tribute to an impression of height and elegance. Let into a

step at the entrance is a plaque of slate dated 1686 and bearing the coat-of-arms of de La Rochefoucauld family who gave six abbesses to the Paraclete.

The house is elegant inside as well as out. Spacious rooms with high ceilings open one into another. Walls are panelled in wood. The stairs are wood. In a *petit salon*, its windows looking to the east, I noticed engravings—some showing the Paraclete in earlier times, others depicting episodes from the lives of Héloïse and Abelard. The dining-room where I sat over a breakfast of lemon-tea, toast, and honey from the comb was suffused with a cool green light cast by trees near enough for one to be pleasantly conscious of their presence yet not so near as to make the interior gloomy. Their branches swayed in the breeze. Birds twittered. And in the distance I heard the laughter of children.

"There is not a great deal to see," M. le Baron remarked in polished English as we went down the steps, then along a path under the trees. This was true had I come hoping to see spectacular ruins. But to sense the past, to feel its impact, as distinct from making an historical study or assessment, is not wholly a matter of stone or bricks or archeological finds. While it would be absurd to minimise the impact made upon the senses by the temple of Sunium standing up above a wine-dark sea; or by Petra's blood-red tombs, there is, none the less, another less dramatic, but no less genuine, realisation of the past; one that is simpler in kind and elusive in that it is valid for one person and not another, at one time and not another. Asphodels flowering on an Aegean hillside can do more than recall the world of Homer—for a fleeting moment his world and ours are one. Once, when a cock crowed as the stars paled above the domes of Jerusalem, I was not reminded of the hours preceding the first Good Friday—I was there, with Peter, in the courtyard of the High Priest's palace. Moreover, in places where there are ancient trees, the past lives with a particular intensity. The sighing of the wind in the leaves; the creaking of a branch; the scent wafted from blossom, foliage, or bark; the thought of great roots plunging deep into the earth—these stir the imagination, release it from the trammels of the present moment.

To the north of the château near the de Roucy garden (so named after Marie-Charlotte de La Rochefoucauld de Roucy, the last abbess of the Paraclete) is the Arduzon, its waters green alike from the profusion of weed swaying in its depth and from the shadow of trees that grow on either bank to the river's edge. Low down, close to the water, is an ancient stone arch almost adjoining what formerly was a mill, but is now a summer residence—a small charming house that might have come out of a tale of romance or a fairy-tale. It was here, where the mill had stood, that Abelard built out of reeds and thatch his oratory in honour of the Trinity, hoping that in this place of seclusion he would find respite from his persecutors. It was here that his students having come in search of him rebuilt the oratory with stones and timber. It was in this same oratory—by this time an abbey dedicated to the Holy Spirit, the Comforter—that Héloïse and her nuns offered prayers (some of them can be read to this day) on Abelard's behalf, first of all in his presence, when he was at the Paraclete while establishing the convent, and later in his absence when he had returned to Brittany to the monastery at Saint-Gildas-de-Rhuys. Here Peter the Venerable, at the wish of Héloïse, laid "the body of the master", having brought it from Saint-Marcel. And here, after twenty years had passed, Héloïse was herself buried along with him whom she had called her master, lover, husband; her father and her brother in Christ. That was in May 1164. A little over three hundred years later, on May 2nd, 1497, Catherine III de Courcelles, abbess of the Paraclete, had the bodies of the founder and the first abbess[16] removed from their original resting place to

a larger church that, within a hundred years of the death of
Héloïse, had been built further back from the river, to the
south. According to the documents of the times, the bones
were taken from what had come to be known as *le petit
moustier*, the "little monastery" (to distinguish it from the
new church), "a damp, watery spot", *loco humido et aquoso*,
and were buried in what was now the abbey church, on either
side of the high altar—those of Abelard on the right and those
of Héloïse on the left.

In the year 1621 under the abbacy of Marie III de La
Rochefoucauld (the first abbess to belong to this family) the
bones were again moved, this time to the crypt under the
apse. A note in the necrology of the Paraclete says that they
were buried under the high altar. Two Benedictines, however, Dom Martène and Dom Durand, of the community of
Saint-Maur, who have left a record of a visit they paid the
Paraclete in the early years of the seventeen hundreds, declare
that the bones were buried not under the high altar, but in a
side-chapel in the crypt "behind the choir and under the
bells", below an altar on which rested a statue representing
the Three Persons of the Trinity, that had been carved in the
twelfth century from a single stone, under the direction of
Abelard. This statue, the same Benedictines relate, was
moved in 1701 by order of the abbess Catherine IV de La
Rochefoucauld (at the suggestion of persons who thought it
deserved a more conspicuous position) out of the crypt to the
choir. The intention was that the bones of Héloïse and Abelard should rest under it in its new position, and an elaborate
inscription to this effect was composed in French and put in
place. Despite this, the bones remained for the time being
where they were. They were reburied under the statue of the
Trinity only in 1780, in the abbacy of Marie-Charlotte de La
Rochefoucauld de Roucy—not however in the choir as previously intended but in a new position in the crypt, under the

apse. There they remained until 1792, when the abbey was sold and the monastic buildings, with the exception of the residence of the abbess, demolished. Some days before the sale the bones were taken in solemn procession to the church of Saint-Laurent at Nogent-sur-Seine, from where they were removed to Paris in 1800, first to the Musée des Monuments Français, in the rue des Petits-Augustins, founded by Alexandre Lenoir, and afterwards to Mont-Louis, now Père-Lachaise.

On the site of the abbey church—and taking the place of a bakery constructed in 1793—is a chapel built by the father of the present owner of the château; and below this, running the nave's length, a cavern forming part of the crypt of the original church. A little to the east of the chapel, on raised ground planted with shrubs, an obelisk set up in 1821 by General Pajol, then owner of the property, marks the position of a second smaller cavern, part of the same crypt and directly under what would have been the apse. It was here, in this second cavern, that the bones of Héloïse and Abelard rested below the statue of the Trinity.

The grandchildren of M. le Baron went with me along the curving tree-shadowed path that led to the entrance of the cavern. The face of the girl at my side had a quiet, grave beauty; it brought to my mind a face I had seen in a mediaeval carving. The three little boys went in front, their hair smooth and black, their plump legs, bare below bright-coloured shorts, a deep olive brown. Their voices rang out in chatter and laughter. From time to time the smallest looked round, his black eyes sparkling, his face wreathed in a smile. At the entrance to the cavern a silence fell. The girl stood back, the boys gathered round, one of them holding a lighted torch. Bending down, I went in. There was a damp smell and overhead a low vaulted roof of rough, pallid stones. On the ground was a granite slab marked at each corner with a small cross.

On this had rested the sarcophagus containing the bones of Héloïse and Abelard.

I came out again to the sunlight and the laughter of the children.

During the period immediately following the death of Héloïse in 1164 the number of religious at the Paraclete had continued to increase. In 1196 a complaint was made to the Pope that the abbey was being compelled to admit more postulants than it could provide for, after which the number was limited to sixty. In 1359, during the wars with the English, the abbey was almost entirely destroyed and the religious dispersed. However, at the end of the century Pope Benedict XIII was asking for contributions from the faithful towards its restoration, with the consequence that in a short while it was once more flourishing. Its history none the less continued to be a chequered one. In 1605 a fire caused widespread damage to the farm buildings which were restored some years later under the direction of the Abbess Marie III de La Rochefoucauld. Then in 1650 a storm brought down part of the steeple which in its fall damaged the church.

The Paraclete as it was a short time before the Revolution is depicted in an elegant eighteenth-century painting by Bruandet, engraved by Picquenot and dedicated to Catherine-Marie de La Rochefoucauld de Roucy, the last abbess of a line which had begun with Héloïse. It is shown as a solid building surmounted by a steeple, with many windows, and partly concealed by an avenue of chestnut-trees. Behind are flat-topped hills. The slender steeple tipped by a weather-vane, floating clouds, birds in flight—these accentuate a wide expanse of sky. In the foreground there are haymakers, a covered wagon drawn by two horses, cows grazing. The scene evokes the heat and stillness and the scents of a day in summer.

In 1792, after the Revolution, the religious were dispersed for the second time, the property sold and, with the exception of the residence of the lady abbess (the present château), the buildings demolished. The château passed through a number of hands. For a while it was owned by a lawyer, then by a dealer in old clothes, *un fripier*; then by Boutet de Monvel, the comedian. In 1811 it was bought by General Pajol. After the 1830 revolution it was acquired by M. le Baron Charles Walckenaer, sub-prefect of Nogent-sur-Seine and son of the scholar and man of letters Charles-Athanase Walckenaer, since when it has passed from father to son to the present owner, M. le Baron François Walckenaer.

If the Paraclete is no longer the religious house intended by its founder, neither is it a museum nor an historical curiosity. It is a home and one lived in with graciousness and dignity by persons who esteem its past. It is, moreover, a place of seclusion and tranquillity, as is fitting. For in the first instance it was for Abelard a haven of peace away from the turmoil of Saint-Denis—the place where later, after he had installed Héloïse and her nuns, he would have chosen, had the choice been his, to end his days; and where he had asked that his body might rest in death. For Héloïse it was the only home that was to be hers from the hands of her husband: Abelard had travelled half across France to put it into her keeping. And she, making the best of circumstances beyond her power to change, gave her mind, for his sake, to furthering the welfare of the abbey and later to the establishing of daughter-houses. Deprived of her child, she reared, in Abelard's words, "children to the Lord". Abbesses of distinction followed her, but the Paraclete remained the abbey of Héloïse, and is remembered as such to this day.

In the company of the grandchildren I saw the farm, a few

minutes to the south of the château and separated from it by an imposing pinkish-cream wall at either end of which is a sturdy bulging tower topped with a slate roof the shape of a candle-snuffer. A huge square yard is set about by stables, barns, a wine press, a mill, a pigeon-house. Most of these belong to the seventeenth century. But there is a granary far older, built of dark-grey stone and blotched with mustard-yellow lichen. Great buttresses reach out either side of the entrance and a window stands up from the roof. Once the abbey wine-press, it is believed to go back to the days of Héloïse. Beyond the yard, to the south, on the far side of a road that runs between Quincey and Ferreux, the countryside stretches away. The sun was shining on burnished corn, crimson poppies and far-off hills. The air was fragrant. Larks sang.

As we came back from the farm we stopped to look at a fourteenth-century well. Formerly in the yard, it has been brought nearer to the château, where it makes a pleasing ornament. Carved from a single stone it is octagonal on the outside, rounded inside. It is decorated with the head of a gargoyle. From out of it long polished leaves of heart's-tongue ferns reached up to the light.

CHAPTER X

Sous la déférence de la religieuse, elle cacha le dévouement de la femme.

Charles de Rémusat, *Abélard*

Rosa carnis mortificande.

[The rose of passion denied]

Sigebert of Gembloux.

WHEN asking Abelard to compose a Rule for the Paraclete, Héloïse touches on aspects of the religious life which Teresa of Avila, four hundred years later, was to treat of at length. Like Teresa, Héloïse is an advocate of discretion and good sense; like her, she is concerned with essentials. In stressing that the purpose of the religious life is above all else to be a Christian and not more than a Christian—that is, to live, in accordance with the precepts set forth in the Gospels —she anticipates the saying of Teresa that our mistakes come from one source, a failure to keep our eyes fixed on Christ our Lord. Teresa would have endorsed (she did so by implication) the point made by Héloïse that a Rule should not be too exacting; since, if it is, those subject to it, as soon as they fall short on one score, becoming discouraged, give up all. Teresa would have agreed, too, with the distinction between essentials and what Héloïse classifies as *indifferentia*—in regard to the latter Teresa allowed a wide latitude and expected others to do the same: she told the prioress at Seville to eat meat for her health's sake, and thought it ridiculous that the ageing Fra Antonio should go barefoot.

Héloïse and Teresa were also alike in that each was genuinely concerned for the welfare of those for whom she felt herself, as superior, responsible. They were both aware, out of their own experience, of the corruption that could exist in religious houses, but being intelligent and compassionate they realised that this could be the result less of evil intent than force of circumstance. Something of the sort was in the mind of Héloïse when she deplored the lot of those who, having embraced the religious life, found themselves with no sense of direction and no one to set them on their way. Equally, Teresa felt compassion for girls who were enclosed in convents because their fathers could not provide the dowry requisite for what was looked upon as a good marriage. The fact that on such matters Héloïse and Teresa had similar views may in part have to do with their own entry into religion, different in each case though this was. We cannot know what forebodings may have already tormented Héloïse when, to protect her from Fulbert's fury, her husband took her, clad in a nun's habit, to the convent at Argenteuil. What we do know is that on the day of her profession she went to the altar sobbing, the despairing words of Lucan's Cornelia on her lips. Teresa's entry was less agonising, less dramatic. Yet it was not devoid of drama. She made her decision only after a number of emotional crises; and when finally she stole out of her home in a November dawn, to make her way to the convent of the Incarnation, beyond the walls of Avila, her distress at being parted from her father and kinsfolk was such that "the agony of death could not have been greater".

Both for Teresa and Héloïse the distress continued inside the convent. And in each case it was emotional in origin, arising from a warmth of heart—a desire to give and receive affection. Héloïse could not resign herself to separation from Abelard. Still less could she resign herself to an Abelard who, as she saw it, had put between herself and him an infinity of coldness, who betrayed not a hint of tenderness. Teresa missed the companionship of her father, brothers and cousins, and because she was bored frittered away her time, a prey to foolish friendships. For over twenty years she struggled against her natural inclinations, "tossed on a stormy sea".

Victor Cousin, who edited Abelard's works in the nineteenth century, said of Héloïse that she loved like Teresa. Jules Michelet, in his *Histoire de France* published in the same century, is more explicit. Praising disinterested love as exemplified by Héloïse, he says that this was reborn in a spiritual form in Teresa. To say that, whereas Héloïse loved Abelard, Teresa loved God is an oversimplification, but it is true to the extent that, faced with a course of action, Teresa would have asked if it was God's will, Héloïse if it was for Abelard's good. The resemblance between the two is not in the direction taken by their love, but in its intensity, its lack of self-interest and its singleness of purpose. For neither of them, where the beloved was concerned, was any sacrifice too great to be demanded, any obstacle too great to be overcome. They were alike, too, in that they had to an unusual degree an intuitive perception that enabled them to enter into the being of another. The contemplation of Christ's suffering caused Teresa deep distress, while, on the human level, if a friend's head ached, her own, she used to say, ached in sympathy. It was this quality which caused Héloïse to experience Abelard's sufferings as though they were hers; which gave her the strength, against her inclination, to "set a bridle" on her lips that he might have peace of mind.

Teresa, whatever difficulties she had to face in the religious life, was living, once she had made the initial choice, as she wanted to live. The pattern was already apparent when as a small child she set off with her brother to seek martyrdom in the land of the Moors, and, frustrated in this, took to playing in her father's garden at being a nun and building convents. Further, the cloister, far from imprisoning her, opened horizons. She had scope for her gifts, an outlet for her boundless energy. In working for her Reform of the Carmelite Order she travelled immense distances, made friends with persons of every status of society from King Philip II to muleteers. She discussed her ideas, practical and spiritual, with the most eminent minds of the day among both clergy and laity. Her output in writing was considerable, varied and distinguished. Yet there is no reason to doubt her sincerity when, on being asked to compose the treatise on prayer that became the *Castillo Interior*, she begged to be allowed to get on with her spinning. Fundamentally she was a practical, down-to-earth person, in her element when giving a hand with the cooking, hammering in nails, making up accounts or managing her brother's finances. Her relationship with God—despite her mystical experiences and her understanding of the mystical state—had a down-to-earth quality. She did not see God only as her Creator and Redeemer; there were moments when she spoke her mind to him bluntly, as if to an equal.

Teresa's knowledge was partly intuitive, partly the result of an enquiring mind and a highly developed power of observation. In the academic sense she had little education. By comparison, Héloïse was an intellectual. In the words of Peter the Venerable she was a *vere philosophica mulier* [a woman truly devoted to philosophy]. At an age when Teresa was reading mainly romantic tales of chivalry or an occasional spiritual work from her father's library, Héloïse was studying the writers of classical Rome, devoting herself determinedly to the pursuit of knowledge. She was living, too, in a milieu that was predominantly intellectual, in earshot of the school of Notre-Dame. The Paraclete, in the lonely countryside by the Arduzon, was a desert by comparison. There were no scholars there now, no students, as there had been when Abelard first built his oratory and young men had come in pursuit of him. Moreover, the Rule established by Abelard imposed long hours of silence, and, at such times as this was relaxed, Héloïse, who in her uncle's home had heard ideas exchanged by persons of mature mind, was, for the most part, with young girls (*parvulae* is the word Abelard uses) whom it was her task to instruct. Any intellectual life was what she herself made—primarily through studying the Scriptures or the Fathers, and by teaching her nuns Latin or a smattering of Greek or Hebrew. The outside world penetrated from time to time. There had been Abelard's visits at the beginning. And there was the visit of Saint Bernard. Others came, too; for Abelard says that clergy and laity sought out Héloïse. Moreover, in the Rule, the question of who is to be admitted, who sent away, is discussed at length. There was also the occasional letter. Apart from those of Abelard, and later of Peter the Venerable, there are two written to Héloïse by Hugues Métel, a canon of Saint-Augustine, who (he told Saint Bernard) made a practice of writing to persons whom he considered important in the hope of lifting himself above the mediocrity of the circle in which he moved. His florid compositions (of little value in themselves) point to the renown in which the abbess of the Paraclete was held. Having commended her piety, he praises her skill as a versifier—her capacity for putting together "familiar words in a manner unfamiliar"; words "sweeter than honey from the honey comb" that are "the mirror" of her understanding.

As a superior, Teresa of Avila was in her element. She was a natural leader. She liked getting others to put her ideas into practice; and because she was good-humoured and did not stand on her dignity she was successful. But what sort of a superior was Héloïse? According to Abelard she was exemplary—first at Argenteuil where, probably after three years, she became prioress, and later as abbess of the Paraclete. She was capable, gentle, sympathetic, patient, held in affection by religious, sought after by the laity. Abelard had reason to present her in a favourable light: it was necessary to his peace of mind (since he was responsible for her situation) to be able to reassure himself that he had done well in insisting that she should take the veil. This in itself would be enough to throw doubt on the validity of his picture, were it not that what he says is corroborated by Peter the Venerable who praises, in yet more glowing terms, this abbess who by her example and courage has raised "a tabernacle precious in the sight of the Lord"—regretting only that she is not in a Cluniac convent. Likewise, papal bulls and charters bear witness to the veneration in which she was held; and the chroniclers are unanimous in praise of her wisdom, prudence, and piety. Again, in the necrology of the Paraclete the entry for May 16th runs: *Mater nostre religionis Heloisa, prima abbatissa, documentis et religione clarissima, spem bonam eius nobis vita donante, feliciter migravit ad Dominum.* [Héloïse the first abbess and mother of our religious house, renowned for her learning and spirituality, having by her life given us good hope, has departed happily to the Lord.] And this finds an echo in a French calendar: *Héloïse, mère et première abbesse de céans, de doctrine et religion très resplendissante.* [Héloïse, mother and first abbess of this house, a light of learning and spirituality.] In her epitaph she is the "prudent Heloise": *Hoc tumulo abbatissa jacet prudens Heloisa.* [The wise Heloise rests in this tomb.]

Prudens. The English derivative does not fully convey the discretion, good sense and judgement implicit in the Latin— qualities particularly evident, when she is writing to Abelard about the Rule, in her awareness of the difficulties of the religious life and her desire to alleviate these, while at the same time setting before her community a nobler ideal. Moreover whereas Abelard was on bad terms with his monks, Héloïse is plainly in sympathy with her companions: there is no suggestion of discord. A nun against her nature, she could have become a self-centred, neurotic; Teresa of Avila was familiar with nuns of this kind. Instead, despite anguish of mind, Héloïse interested herself in others and used her intellectual gifts for their betterment. And it was the harder for her because, unlike Teresa, she was conditioned neither by temperament nor by the circumstances of earlier life to devote herself to a group or cause, but to an individual. Yet, because she was not swamped by emotion, she turned her love for Abelard to the advantage of all, enabling her nuns and not herself alone to reap the fruits of his intellect. While his relationship to her remained unique, he was in a real sense the father and director of the community.

There is no doubt as to the impression made by the abbess of the Paraclete upon others. The picture she herself gives is a different one. While conceding to Abelard that she appears well in the eyes of the world, this, she insists with a fiery vehemence, means that she is a hypocrite. Outwardly all may be well, but God knows otherwise: he knows that she conforms only because circumstances force her to do so. At heart she is neither resigned nor submissive, but rebellious. Her life of penance, however hard it be, is unavailing in the sight of God, because she cannot accept as just the punishment visited upon Abelard at the time when he, through the marriage, had done all in his power to make amends; nor, when she should be lamenting her past, can she cease to long for what she has lost. A false exterior, whether her own or that of others, is repellent to Héloïse. It is impossible to read her letters without detecting from time to time a note of disillusion on this score in her attitude not to religion, but to the practice of it.

It is in the first letter when she writes of clerics who had known how to receive offerings, but not to make them; whose hands had been ready to take, but not to give: *manus ad suscipiendum non ad dandum habuerant*. And in the second, when she says that in her century there is little religion that is not tainted with hypocrisy: *parva pars religionis non est hypocrisis*. In her personal life religion, or what passed as such, had not been kind to Héloïse and it may be that this (without her knowing it) left its mark. An ideal in part philosophical, in part religious—in either case emanating from Saint Jerome—had dictated the arguments that she had used against the marriage. The same ideal was at the root of Abelard's attempt to conceal the marriage; and her own denial that it had taken place, followed (as a consequence of this denial) by the maltreatment of her by Fulbert. Then, after she had been constrained by Abelard to take refuge at Argenteuil, a wife in nun's garments, this same uncle (a canon of the church and as such committed in an especial way to God's service) had wreaked on her husband the barbarous vengeance. And as though that were not enough, there had been Abelard's decision to take himself to Saint-Denis, having first seen to it that she became a nun at Argenteuil. After nine years at Argenteuil, Suger, abbot of Saint-Denis, had driven her out of the convent.

There are words written by Héloïse which, if wrested from their context, might appear flippant, even brazen. And yet they are neither. In laying bare her innermost thoughts she is appealing both to her husband, at whose word she consented to become a religious, and to her father in Christ, from whom she has the right to guidance. Moreover, her vehemence is not simply an expression of personal unhappiness: it has the further twofold purpose of rousing Abelard from a self-absorption beneficial neither to himself nor her and of proving to him that, though others may reject him, her devotion is unchanged. What Abelard calls her "complaint" (reading into her words, because his conscience is ill at ease, an accusation) has nothing in common with the lament of a nun of the same century:

Heu misella!
Nihil deterius
Tali vita

[What a poor, unhappy creature I am! Nothing could be worse than such a life!]

The helplessness and self-pity evoked by the use of the diminutive (*misella*) are not in the spirit of Héloïse who was resourceful and proud: they have more in common with the unfortunate Marianne, the Portuguese nun who (some four centuries later) writing to le comte de Chamilly, decries "this wretched cloister", *ce malheureux cloître*, where she has been enclosed among "disagreeable persons" since childhood. The abbess of the Paraclete, unlike the nun of her own century who was voicing her lament to no one in particular, unlike Marianne, who was writing to her lover, addresses her husband. Unlike Marianne, Héloïse had not been put into a convent when a child—by comparison she was mature when she entered; and if the decision was not what she would have wished, nevertheless she had made it herself, knowing precisely why she was doing so. Again unlike Marianne, she has nothing to say against the convent as such. For Marianne it was a prison from which she wanted only to escape and where she had no scruples about receiving surreptitiously her lover with his flattering words and his trinkets. Héloïse, too, was imprisoned. "The walls of ice," as Chateaubriand has said, "stand up about her": *s'élèvent des murs glacés.* Yet it is not a prison from which she asks to escape. For it is within these walls, in the framework of this life, that she has committed herself to prove her devotion to her husband.

God is absent from the letters of Marianne. He presents no problem since, as far as she is concerned, he can scarcely be said to exist. If she could be united by any means to her

lover, all, she supposes, would be well. She is prepared to leave
the convent, abandon the life of religion, if she can but re-
join him. Héloïse, on the contrary, asks that Abelard shall restore himself to her "in such a manner as is possible"—that
is, she continues, by his presence at his own foundation or by
a letter. The question of her leaving the convent does not
arise. God is real to Héloïse: her very indignation against
him bears this out. What Marianne calls her *passion* is her entire existence. Héloïse, though Abelard is the centre of her
life and the mainspring of her decisions and actions, lives on
more than one level. An awareness of God gives depth and
perspective to her thought. If she complains of God's cruelty
to Abelard, she also sees God as his protector—in so far as
there is any to protect him. Abelard is the founder of the
Paraclete, but under God. In the divine dispensation the vineyard is Abelard's, but it is God who shall give the increase.
When she says that having done nothing for God, she can
expect nothing from him, this is an expression of the predicament in which she finds herself, committed, by reason of her
"supreme act of folly" (her folly in consenting to become a
nun and thus be parted from her husband), to a way of
life for which she has no calling. For whereas for Abelard,
though he admits having entered Saint-Denis without a vocation, the religious life has become at least to some degree a protection and an alibi, for Héloïse it remains what it
has been from the beginning, a burden shouldered for his sake.
But this life, once embraced, brings with it (if only because
otherwise it has no value as the act of reparation to Abelard
that she intends it to be) its obligations. She is committed,
from the day she took the veil from the altar at Argenteuil,
to love in purity of heart a God whom—because she thinks
that to love God means to love him as she does Abelard—she
believes she cannot love. She is committed to serve a God
whom, because she derives no satisfaction in serving him, she

thinks she does not serve. She is committed to pray to a God to whom, because memories and emotions cloud her thoughts, she can pray only with the greatest difficulty.

The impression given by Héloïse is less of one who prays than one who remonstrates with her Creator—or apostrophises him from a long way off. But all she says must be related to the circumstances in which these most unusual letters were written. In any case prayer can take many forms—there are plenty of remonstrations in the Book of Job. As to prayer in the more usual sense, Héloïse saw to it that prayers were offered on behalf of Abelard in the Paraclete and asked him for a psalter for this purpose. In considering the Rule, she puts prayer as the central act of the religious life. Nor would anyone who did not believe in the efficacy of prayer have shown the concern that she did to ensure that the *tricenarium* of Masses promised by Peter the Venerable should be offered on her behalf.

Teresa of Avila's life as a nun was illumined by an awareness of God's presence—this was a matter not of her mystical experiences, but a realisation of Providence working in day-to-day happenings. She was not in the dilemma of Héloïse who had brought with her into the convent a passionate and exclusive human love, the object of which was her own husband, for whose sake alone she had consented to take the veil. For Héloïse, Abelard and her life as a religious were inseparably linked. She had become a nun not to thrust human love into the past, but to prove its reality in the present. The present had not taken the place of the past. Nor had the cloister become for her a substitute for Abelard. In the one person, there is Héloïse the nun and Héloïse the wife of Abelard. As she says in her superscription, the nun belongs to God, the wife to Abelard. Charles de Rémusat in what amounts to a commentary on these words writes: *Héloïse se conforma aux volontés d'Abélard et pour lui à tous les devoirs de son état. Sous la déférence de la religieuse, elle cacha le dévouement de la femme . . . inconsolable et indomptée, elle obéit et ne se soumit pas; elle accepta tous ses devoirs, sans en faire beaucoup de cas, et son âme n'aima jamais ses vertus.* [Héloïse complied with the wishes of Abelard and for his sake she accomplished all the duties of her state. The deference of the nun hid the devotion of the wife. Inconsolable and unconquered she obeyed and did not give in. She accepted all her duties without making much of them, and in her heart she found no pleasure in her virtues.] That is to say, with a fortitude worthy of her Stoic mentors Héloïse endured the austerities and deprivations of the religious life without (so she believed) the grace requisite to her state, since having become a religious from no supernatural motive she merited no such grace—to support her, she had only the love that she bore her husband.

What would Teresa of Avila have thought of Héloïse had the two met across the centuries? Impatient of stupidity, insistent that her novices should be intelligent, filled with admiration for learning when she met it in men and quick to deplore the lack of it in women, would she have admired the intellectual qualities in Héloïse or would she have viewed her with suspicion as she did a highbrow young woman who came one day, Bible in hand, asking to be a Carmelite? Teresa was shrewd in her judgements, and she found the young woman pretentious. But there was nothing pretentious about Héloïse. Teresa would have recognised this. As to Héloïse in her role as abbess of the Paraclete, Teresa would have looked beyond words to actions: she warns her friend Padre Gracián against the folly of supposing he could know his women penitents solely from what they told him about themselves. Teresa would have appreciated, as did Peter the Venerable, the magnitude of the sacrifice that Héloïse had

made, as well as all that she had done for the welfare of the
Paraclete and its daughter-houses. A natural psychologist, she
would have agreed with Etienne Gilson who, speaking for our
own psychologically minded age, says that Héloïse did not
know everything about her own situation: *Héloïse elle-même
n'a pas tout su de son propre cas.* For whereas on the human
level the perception of Héloïse in regard to both herself and
Abelard was remarkable, she did not think of herself as living
a spiritual life, since what she did, she did for Abelard. It did
not enter her mind (so far as her writings indicate) to presume that what she was doing for him she was also doing for
God. Abelard loomed too large for her to see beyond. She
could not see God working through Abelard (grace working
through the channels of nature); sanctifying her through Abelard; through a human love which (though she did not know
this and so was protected from any shadow of complacency)
was also love of God who, being himself love, is the source of
love. She knew the choice she had made for Abelard's sake
and why she had made it, but she did not see beyond this.

Persons without any particular religious belief are generally
content to accept that the devotion of Héloïse to her husband
enabled her to endure her life as a nun. It is to certain of the
religious-minded (those who scale-down God's grace to the
limitations of their own vision) that Héloïse can be a source
of embarrassment, in that they cannot fit her into any cate-
gory of virtue as they know it. The nun who sings the praises
of a heavenly Spouse, whose peace of heart is undisturbed by
human affection, they understand. But Héloïse who has on
her lips no song of praise for her Creator but only for him who
once had been her lover and is still her husband; yet who,
despite this, carries out the duties of her state in a manner
that is beyond reproach—this does not conform to the commonly accepted pattern of things as they ought to be. To attempt to understand Héloïse calls for breadth of vision[17]—a

realisation that there can be no rigid distinction between love
of God and human love; that love can have two directions
and yet ultimately be one: *duo praecepta, sed una charitas.*
Viewed in the light of the Gospels Héloïse does not present
a problem. For on the last day, who are they who are to be
singled out as the ones whom the King shall call to himself?
Not (strange though this may seem) those who have know-
ingly served him and therefore might legitimately expect to
be summoned. But others who, because they have no knowledge of having rendered any such service, will be amazed to
be chosen. "When Lord?" will be the burden of their as-
tonished cry. "Lord, *when* saw we thee an hungered and fed
thee? Or thirsty, and gave thee to drink? *When* saw we thee a
stranger, and took thee in? Or naked, and clothed thee? Or
when saw we thee sick, or in prison, and came unto thee?"
And the King shall answer: "Verily I say unto you, inasmuch
as ye have done it unto one of the least of these my brethren,
ye have done it unto me."

CHAPTER XI

"Each century re-creates the figures of the past
in the light of its own vision."

DURING the period following her death Héloïse is remembered in the documents of the Paraclete and in the
chroniclers as the abbess who ruled over her convent with
wisdom and holiness: *prudenter atque religiose rexit*. As to
Abelard, the chronicles for the most part confirm what is apparent in the correspondence. He is the brilliant philosopher,
the master of the schools, sharp of wit, subtle of intellect;
distinguished alike as a writer and a teacher. He is also ar-
rogant, presumptuous, a stirrer-up of contention, so filled with
pride in his own powers that he cannot listen to the opinion
of another. In the chronicle of Saint-Gildas-de-Rhuys, his own
monastery, he is dismissed with a curt reference to the "run-
away abbot", *abbas fugitivus*, who died in 1142.

As to the personal story of these two, the little that is said
(there are references, for example, to Fulbert's vengeance)
presupposes the facts to be familiar to the reader. There are
however two passages that stand apart. The Godel Chronicle
(attributed to Guillaume Godel, a monk of Saint-Martial-de-
Limoges, but believed to be the work of an Englishman who
entered the cloister in 1144) after recording how Abelard put
at the head of the nuns of the Paraclete Héloïse his wife, who
as well as being holy was versed in Latin and Hebrew, adds
(making a play on the word *amica*) that she who was in very
truth his friend, *vere ipsius amica*, continued after his death
to prove her friendship by offering prayers unremittingly on
his behalf. Then in the Tours Chronicle of the following

century there is the legend telling how, when after her death
the body of Héloïse was brought to be laid at her husband's
side, Abelard reached out his arms to receive her.

Apart from Walter Map's lines evoking the bewilderment
of the bride when her husband enters the cloister, the first
recognition of Héloïse and Abelard in literature is in the
Roman de la Rose, in a passage that outlines the story, then
dwells at length on the objections raised by Héloïse against
the marriage. Indeed at one time the *Roman de la Rose* was
attributed to Abelard—on the grounds of the eulogy contained
in it of Héloïse. The lines were in fact written more than a
hundred years after Abelard's death by Jean de Meung, the
first person to translate the letters of Héloïse and Abelard
into French. Cynical, scornful of women, he nonetheless admired Héloïse, into whose arguments against the marriage he
read a point of view that was his own rather than hers. But
his admiration was sincere. For him she was *la saige Heloys*—
the nobility of her character had stunned him, despite himself,
into admiration:

> *Mai je me crei mie par m'ame,*
> *Qu'onques puis fust nul tel fame.*

[Upon my soul I do not believe that there has ever been
such a woman.]

It was probably through the *Roman de la Rose* that
Chaucer, writing in the following century, was familiar with:

> "Helowys
> That was abbesse nat fer fro Parys."

Roughly contemporary with Chaucer was Petrarch, poet
and humanist. In the Bibliothèque Nationale I held in my
hand a manuscript of the letters of Héloïse and Abelard that
once had been his—one of seventeen manuscripts brought to

France from Pavia by Louis XII. It is written on parchment in a neat Gothic hand. The capital S (picked out in blue and crimson) at the opening of the *Historia Calamitatum* encloses, against a backcloth of gold-leaf, the figures of a monk and nun wearing the black Benedictine habit, seated side by side. The head of the nun (the face is blotted out) is inclined in the direction of the monk. An open book rests on their knees. On the fly-leaf of the manuscript is a list of contents in faded ink, and underneath the words: *putantur hec scripta manu D.F. Petrarchae* [these are thought to be written by the hand of Master Francesco Petrarch]. Then follows his name; and, again in a different hand, *fuit*, meaning that the manuscript was formerly his. In the margins there are signs (sometimes it is a pointing finger) and comments drawing attention to a passage or phrase in the text, believed to be written by the poet. His observations are not those of a scholar, but of one who identifies himself emotionally with what he is reading, sometimes linking an episode from the letters with an occurrence in his own life. When Abelard writes of his fall from a horse, Petrarch says: *et me nocte,* referring to the night on which he was thrown near Reggio, when his horse stumbled. As he reads the letters of Héloïse, he shares and applauds her sentiments. When she explains her motive in becoming a nun, adding that she wanted of Abelard nothing other than himself, Petrarch writes: *Valde predulciter ac blande per totum agis Heloysa;* meaning that her entire attitude is one of tenderness and graciousness. When she says that she would have followed or preceded Abelard into hell; and that, if there was any doubt as to her motives at the beginning, the end has proved her intention, he writes: *amicissime et eleganter,* showing pleasure at her warmth of feeling, but also at the grace with which she expresses herself. As I turned over the pages that Petrarch had turned, read the words that he had written, I felt myself entering into his experience of the letters, and this in turn was enriching my own. Are, then, the letters not sufficient in themselves? Do they need another's comments? A beautiful woman does not need jewels. Yet jewels can enhance her beauty.

Some hundred years after Petrarch the thoughts of another poet were to turn to Héloïse. François Villon in the spring of 1461, when he was ill and preoccupied with the approach of death, let his mind rove to the transient brightness of other days. Echoing Jean de Meung's *saige Heloys* he writes in the *Ballade des Dames du Temps Jadis*:

> *Où est la très sage Héllois*
> *Pour qui fut chastré, puis moine,*
> *Pierre Esbaillart à Saint-Denis?*
> *Pour son amour eut cette essoyne . . .*
> *Mais où sont les neiges d'antan?*

[Where is the most wise Héloïse, on whose account Peter Abelard was castrated then became a monk at Saint-Denis? For his love he suffered this ill fortune . . . But where are the snows of yester-year?]

A mention here and there in documents and chronicles; Walter Map's verses; sixty-four lines in the *Roman de la Rose*; a line and a half in Chaucer's prologue to *The Wife of Bath's Tale*; Petrarch's annotations; Villon's lines—these do not amount to much. In his own day Abelard's mutilation and the happenings leading up to and following it made an immediate sensation that had repercussions far beyond Paris. But what is news on one day is often forgotten the next. And in this instance there was probably some deliberate forgetting. The manuscripts of the letters were few and in the keeping of the monasteries; and their content not the most suitable for transcription in the libraries of religious houses. Not that the monks were prudish—after all, they transcribed Ovid's *Ars Amandi*. Nevertheless it is understandable that there may have been a tendency to suppress rather than publicise the onslaught made by Abelard against clerics, some of whom were in high places.

Yet this is not enough to explain the relative indifference shown to the story of Héloïse and Abelard in a period when tales of love were in vogue to a degree hitherto unknown— in the twelfth century there were as many as twenty versions of the Tristan and Iseult myth. A more probable explanation is to be found in the nature of their story, which does not conform to the tradition of courtly love as popularised by the troubadours and the Cathars (the latter founded a Church of Love in contradistinction to the Church of Rome), the two originating in Provence and extending their influence simultaneously. The first troubadour, William sixth count of Poitiers and ninth duke of Aquitaine, died in 1127. The earliest reference to an organised Cathar Church dates from 1160, but the teaching of the Cathars, which was Manichaean in its origins—in particular its condemnation of the flesh and consequently of marriage—had already found acceptance, especially in Orléans, Poitou, and Aquitaine. In *cortezia* or courtly love there is a distance between lover and beloved. The man is the servant of the woman, a knight kneeling at the feet of his lady who is remote, cold, inflexible. He is at her mercy, abject in the face of her rebukes, asking nothing of her but that he may satisfy her slightest whim. There is no dialogue between them. No reality in their relationship. As the writer of the *Roman de la Rose* has put it: "Of *donnoi* [the Provençal word for the relationship between a knight and his lady] he knows nothing who wants fully to possess his lady." Marriage being despised, chastity is exalted into a fetish, with the resultant paradox that (since one extreme breeds the opposite, and repression in one direction seeks an outlet in another) adultery no less than chastity becomes a mark of courtly love. Moreover in *cortezia* there is obstruction. This must be so, since the lovers do not love each other, but the pain of their unsatisfied passion which they hug to themselves—for were this pain to be removed they would have nothing left to love. Tristan and Iseult do not love each other: they love the passion imposed upon them by the drinking of the love-potion. Tristan admits this when he is talking to the hermit Ogrin. And Iseult confirms that it is so:

> Sire, por Deu omnipotent,
> Il ne m'aime pas, ne je lui,
> Fors par un herbé dont je bui,
> Et il en but . . .

[Sir, by Almighty God, he does not love me nor I him, except for a potion which I drank and he drank.]

Though Abelard extolled Héloïse in song in the manner of a courtly lover extolling his lady; though certain aspects of their love justify their being cited as "the earliest passionate lovers whose story has reached us", though one can point not merely to one but to a series of obstructions, whether these be regarded as self-imposed or as coming from without; and it might be argued that for them the cloister was the equivalent of the sword that lay between Tristan and Iseult—even so their story does not conform to the pattern of courtly love. Héloïse is not cold, distant, inflexible, but warm and outgoing. She does not exact a slavish service from Abelard—it is she who serves him, considering his wishes, setting his welfare before her own. Moreover love finds physical expression. And there is a marriage, strange though its circumstances. Further, whereas in *cortezia* love and death are coupled ("My lords, if you would hear a high tale of love and death", are the opening words of Bedier's *Tristan and Iseult*), these two lived on, each to answer a need in the other and to see their first passion not die but become transmuted, as near as could be within the limitation of tempera-

ment, character, and circumstance, into "a winnowed purity". These are not figures taken out of *littérature courtoise*,
but creatures of flesh and blood.

If the Middle Ages showed comparatively little interest in
Héloïse and Abelard, the same cannot be said of the sixteen
hundreds. In 1616 Abelard's works, including the correspondence but omitting the hymns, the verses to Astralabe and
the *Hexameron*, were published in Paris in two editions
ascribed to François d'Amboise with notes by André
Duchesne. These were cumbersome, expensive productions,
acceptable to an *élite* but not to a public for the most part
no longer familiar with Latin. But it was not only a matter of
language. The spirit of the letters and of the world in which
they had been written was alien to that of the seventeenth
century. This explains the popularity of works of extravagant
fantasy, but reflecting the mood of the day, that appeared
towards the end of the century. One of these, *Les Amours
d'Abailard et d'Héloïse* by Jacques Alluis, a lawyer of
Grenoble, was published at Amsterdam in 1695. It contained a romanticised version of the original events, translations of some of the letters and a paraphrase of the *Historia
Calamitatum* under the title *Lettre d'Abailard à Philinthe*.
In the same year a somewhat similar version by Du Bois had
the title *Histoire des Amours et Infortunés d'Abélard et
d'Eloïse*. In 1697 there appeared, filled out with fictional
episodes, what was supposed to be a translation of the first
two letters of Héloïse with Abelard's reply to the earlier of
them—the work of Roger de Rabutin, Comte de Bussy, cousin
of Madame de Sévigné who had encouraged him, telling him
that his versions were so delightful that she had neither the
wish nor need to read the originals.

These publications were forerunners of a spate of such
works, some better, some worse, some entertaining, some

tedious, all of them bedevilled with falsifications and in spirit totally alien to the Héloïse and Abelard of the Middle Ages. Abelard has become *un homme de qualité*, a writer not of philosophy but *billets-doux*. Héloïse is *une héroïne gallante et précieuse*, self-centred, affected, sharp-tongued, frivolous.

From time to time a protest was made, but it was scarcely more than a voice in the wilderness. In 1723 Dom Gervaise, a monk of La Trappe, brought out first a life of Abelard, then a translation of the letters. Objecting to the distortions of the day, he declared that it was his intention to "walk the ways of truth". But he, too, though in a different manner, let his imagination run riot. In an understandable zeal to rescue from obloquy and triviality two persons whom he held in high esteem, he allowed himself to embroider the truth; and his version of the letters is less a translation than a flowery paraphrase. It was the translation of Dom Gervaise that the librarian of the abbey of Sainte-Geneviève had in mind when in the mid-seventeen hundreds he wrote on a fly-leaf of a popular edition a word of caution to the effect that the contents were mainly false and that the intending reader would do well to consult instead a "faithful rendering", indicating where on the library shelves a copy of the version by Dom Gervaise was to be found.

Alexander Pope published his *Eloisa to Abelard* in 1717. It is most unlikely that he had read the letters in Latin; copies of the edition brought out by François d'Amboise in 1616 were scarce, and the first Latin version to appear in England was that of Richard Rawlinson in 1718. Pope's source was John Hughes' *Letters of Abelard and Héloïse* published in 1713: a hotch-potch from Roger de Rabutin and others of his kind, translated into English. There is little in common between *la héroïne gallante* of Hughes' version and Pope's weeping abbess, except that each reflects the mood of a century.

For by Pope's day the brittle gaiety of the *Grand Siècle* had
yielded through a very surfeit of itself to a languor that, extending its influence to England, gave birth there, even more
than on the continent, to a studied gloom as artificial as had
been the former gaiety. Moreover in the mood of the century
Pope encountered a melancholy that matched his own. For
he was ill, disillusioned and lonely—the loneliness of one who
cannot forget or believe that others can forget an ever-
present physical debility. *Eloisa to Abelard* came out about
a year after he had made the acquaintance of the spoilt, ar-
rogant Lady Mary Wortley-Montagu to whom he sent a copy
of the poem; and who later, when the two had quarrelled,
mocked the hunchback for having dared to speak to her of
love.

Infusing, therefore, into the Héloïse of his creation his own
solitary pain, he depicts an abbess lost in a convent's gloom,
engulfed in grief, praying for death. This Héloïse is swept
on the surge of her emotions, torn between what she sees
now as love of God, now love of Abelard; she is less clear-
sighted, less intelligent than the Héloïse of the letters, who
was incapable of deceiving herself into supposing that she
wished for:

> the blameless Vestal's lot
> The world forgetting, by the world forgot.

Moreover the arguments used by Pope's Héloïse against the
marriage are not based, as are those in the letters, on consideration for Abelard's welfare, but are an attack on marriage as such. Indeed the marriage itself is so "played down"
that were it not for the line:

> Come thou, my father, brother, husband, friend!

one could forget that there had been a marriage.

Yet there are moments when Pope's heroine speaks with

the authentic voice of Héloïse. She does so perhaps most of all when she recalls to Abelard her motive in entering religion and her continued need for him:

> Not grace, or zeal, love only was my call,
> And if I lose thy love, I lose my all.

Eloisa to Abelard was translated into French in 1758 by the poet Charles-Pierre Colardeau under the title *Lettre d'Héloïse*. It is a lifeless version without the emotion and atmosphere of Pope, but it was popular. From that time a flood of translations and imitations both of this and Pope's original appeared in England, France, Germany, Italy, and Portugal.

Chateaubriand's portrait of Héloïse in *Le Génie du Christianisme*, published in 1801, derives largely from Pope—he quotes from Colardeau but is critical of the latter's *esprit irréligieux*. Chateaubriand's Héloïse is less tearful than Pope's but there is an increased emphasis on what he sees as a conflict between nature and grace: *La religion et l'amour exercent à la fois leur empire sur son cœur*. She is presented as faced with a choice between God and her lover: *il faut qu'elle choisisse entre Dieu et un amant*—and Chateaubriand's God is the jealous God of Sinai (*le Dieu de Sinaï est un Dieu jaloux*) who does not permit her to spare for Abelard a particle of her love. Like Pope, Chateaubriand practically ignores that, monk and nun though they are, these two are also husband and wife—a fact which makes their relationship unique and one which in the original letters is emphasised first by Héloïse and afterwards (when Héloïse has put the idea into his head) even more so by Abelard.

Chateaubrind makes a comparison between the plight of Héloïse and that of Dido. He says that if a Racine had interpreted Héloïse, her sufferings would have surpassed in tragic effect those of the queen of Carthage. And yet, great as were these sufferings, her story viewed in its entirety is less one of tragedy than of victory over circumstances. The tragedy of Dido and Aeneas lay not so much in their parting as in the manner in which they parted. Shocked by what she saw as her lover's betrayal of her, too swamped by emotions to be able to view his behaviour with any degree of detachment, having failed moreover to persuade him to change his purpose, Dido fell back on recriminations, thus widening the gulf separating her from Aeneas and laying in store for herself only bitterness of heart. There was no bond of mutual understanding to hold these two together. When he sailed from Carthage, Aeneas turned his back on Dido, bringing to a close what for him had been a pleasant interlude but hardly more than this. Abelard, however his motives are to be judged, did not turn his back on Héloïse. In insisting that she should be a nun he was drawing into his own life her whom he was determined "to keep forever"; making certain that she would have no life apart from his. Then, having ensured, as far as was possible, that this was so, he subsequently made over to her his only possession: the oratory of the Paraclete; provided her with a Rule, and, from that time, was at pains to carry out her wishes.

Dido was not the only classical heroine with whom Héloïse invited comparison. Another was Alcestis, another Penelope. Alcestis consented to die that her husband might live: Héloïse died in the sense that in becoming a nun she relinquished life as she would have chosen to live it—indeed she equates the cloister with "infernal regions": *Vulcania loca*. A perhaps less obvious resemblance between Euripides' heroine and Héloïse is the indignation felt by each of these wives not at the immensity of the sacrifice required of her, but at the attitude of the husband in taking the sacrifice for granted, as though it were his right.

The traditional Penelope was faithful, patient, wise—all of which attributes can be applied to Héloïse. But for Héloïse fidelity was harder, because the past was, by normal standards, dead; whereas Penelope could hope that, with the return of her husband, the past would be restored. As to patience, if the word be taken in its true sense as meaning not a submissive resignation but a capacity to endure with fortitude what cannot be changed, these women are alike. They are alike again in the wisdom that each displays in applying her intelligence to situations where another would become a prey to emotion. Penelope, when her son speaks sharply to her, resenting that she should treat him as though he were a child, keeps silent; and when her husband returns only to announce that he has another voyage in mind, she shows no resentment. Moreover, the device of the web as a means of keeping the suitors at bay was highly intelligent. Héloïse with a like use of her intelligence adjusted the expression of her love for Abelard to the altered circumstances of their lives.

In the nineteenth century the image of Héloïse has undergone a marked change. *La héroïne gallante* and the weeping abbess are both of the past. The stress now is on selfless devotion as exemplified in the love of a woman for a man, a wife for a husband. Already in the previous century Diderot had exclaimed of Abelard: *comme cet homme fut aimé*; and D'Alembert had told Jean-Jacques Rousseau that if he (Rousseau) thought that women knew neither how to write nor to love, then he had not read the letters of Héloïse, or he had read them in some garbled version. Moreover Rousseau had himself chosen *La Nouvelle Héloïse* as the title of his novel about the love between Julie d'Etanges and her tutor Saint-Preux—in which he tries to reconcile passionate love and virtue. Stendhal in *De l'Amour*, published in 1822, extols the "tender-hearted Heloise": *la tendre Héloïse*. Henri Martin calls her "the great votary of love: *la grande sainte de l'amour*. Jules Michelet, the historian, sees in her the exemplar for all time of selfless love: *On vit pour la première fois dans les lettres d'Héloïse l'immortelle expression du désintéressement et du dévouement sans borne*. Victor Cousin declared that out of all women he would have chosen to be loved by Héloïse. Gabriel Legouvé, in his study *Le Mérite des Femmes*, says that if one woman can symbolise all that is greatest in a wife, that woman is Héloïse: *Si une seule femme peut représenter l'épouse dans sa grandeur c'est Héloïse*.

These voices come for the most part from the Romantics. To recapture the mood of their age one need only reflect on the opening words of Lamartine's study of Abelard: *On n'écrit pas cette histoire, on la chante*. The poet who in his youth had carved verses in honour of Héloïse on a grotto at Clisson admired her no less in his maturity. Love such as hers, he says, can almost be called a virtue: *cet amour se confond presque avec la vertu*.

If these praises are exaggerated to our ears, the nineteenth-century admirers of Héloïse have the merit that, unlike their forerunners of the two preceding centuries, they praise in her qualities that were acknowledged by the chroniclers of her own time; ones, moreover, that are apparent in her correspondence with Abelard and, after his death, in the interchange of letters between herself and Peter the Venerable.

Sometimes Abelard's name is linked with that of Héloïse, the two of them being held in like esteem. But this is rare. In general, in proportion as the glory of Héloïse increases that of Abelard wanes. He is reproached for the seduction of his pupil, for his betrayal of her uncle, and for his vanity. Lamartine, though more sympathetically disposed than many of his contemporaries, says that Abelard was torn in two directions, that he had the courage neither of his passion nor of his reputation: *Abélard flotta entre deux faiblesses, il n'eut ni le courage de sa passion ni celui de sa gloire*. Arsène Houssaye says that it is not on Abelard's own account but through the love bestowed on him by Héloïse that he has achieved immortality.

The writers and scholars of the nineteenth century did more than indulge in romanticism. They went back to the original Latin letters, to the chroniclers and the documents. Charles de Rémusat's biography of Abelard, published in 1845, is a serious and an imaginative study of the philosopher and the man. Moreover the picture it gives of Héloïse is remarkable for its perception, sensitivity, and restraint. Charles de Rémusat had used the Latin text of d'Amboise. In 1849 Victor Cousin brought out a Latin edition of Abelard's works: *Petri Abelardi Opera*, based on the d'Amboise edition but with emendations from other manuscripts. It contained (along with an introduction and notes) all Abelard's writings, including the correspondence with Héloïse, as well as copious documents relevant to their case. This was followed in 1855 by Migne's somewhat similar edition (again the complete works with introduction, notes and documents) compressed into a single close-packed volume in the *Patrologia Latina*.

Charles de Rémusat's *Abélard* is not written from information acquired second-hand. At the beginning of his book the picture he evokes of the straggling street at Le Pallet, the castle ruins and the hill that bears Abelard's name, comes from one whose eyes have looked upon the scene. It had become the fashion to visit places that had associations with Héloïse and Abelard. Artists were attracted by the dramatic scenery at Clisson. Claude Thienon depicted Héloïse, a solitary figure in white, seated in pensive mood under an oak-tree in the park of La Garenne. Prosper Mérimée describes a visit that he made in 1836 to the abbey of Saint-Gildas-de-Rhuys, where he was shown a tunnel leading from the monastery to the sea, by means of which, so he was told, Abelard had escaped from the persecution of his brethren. Visitors to Cluny were shown a lime-tree under which, it was said, Abelard used to sit, his face turned in the direction of the Paraclete; and in the park at Saint-Point Lamartine treasured a table made of stone, at which Abelard was supposed to have written while sitting under the lime-tree. Alexandre Lenoir wrote to a doctor at Saint-Marcel through whom he had acquired the sarcophagus that was believed to be Abelard's, saying that he and his wife wanted to make *un voyage sentimental* to the place where there had rested "the mortal remains of the most grievously afflicted of men". Argenteuil, strangely, appears to have been neglected; indeed that once renowned abbey seems, from the time that it was taken over by Suger, to have slipped out of history.

Throughout the seventeen hundreds pilgrims had come to the Paraclete; and after the bones of Héloïse and Abelard had been taken away (first to the church of Saint-Laurent at Nogent-sur-Seine, then to Paris) they continued to come—lamenting that founder and abbess had been taken away "like gods removed from their shrine", yet happy because "at every step in this time-honoured spot memories were awakened". Tender-hearted devotees, *les âmes sensibles*, came to the house in the rue des Chantres, picturing with emotion the master and the young pupil. Some of them, after the house was pulled down in 1849, mourned the sacrilege that had been committed in demolishing *la vieille maison d'Héloïse*. Others were content with the reconstruction that had taken its place.

But it was the tomb that attracted the largest number of pilgrims. First it was in the Elysée, the garden adjoining the Musée des Monuments Français, to which Lenoir had brought the bones of Héloïse and Abelard from Nogent-sur-Seine in 1804. Napoleon came to see it that year; before going away he left flowers as a tribute to Héloïse, saying that he hoped to return. In 1806 the Empress Josephine was among those who took part in a midnight procession illumined by torches. Then in 1817, after Lenoir's museum had to be disbanded, the tomb was set up anew in the cemetery that is now Père-Lachaise. The bones rested in the sarcophagus from the church of Saint-Marcel, on the lid of which were the recumbent figures of a monk and nun. A plinth supporting the sarcophagus bore the names Héloïse and Abélard, alternating with the words ἀεὶ συμπεπλέγμενοι [united forever]. On the western side of the coffin was the inscription which in the abbacy of Catherine de La Rochefoucauld had been placed in the year 1701 below the statue of the Trinity at the Paraclete.[18] To the left of this were the words: *Le tombeau d'Abélard a été transporté de l'église Saint-Marcel-les-Chalon-sur-Saône en l'an VIII*; to the right: *Les restes d'Héloïse et d' Abélard sont réunis dans ce tombeau.* These words were repeated on the eastern side, on which there was the incorrectly dated inscription: *Les restes d'Abélard et d'Héloïse ont été transportés dans ce lieu en MDCCCXIX.* Enclosing the sarcophagus and rising high above it was an elegant structure, Gothic in style—its slender pillars supporting a roof adorned with gargoyles and soaring spires. Before long an iron railing was put round the tomb to deter pilgrims from cutting their names on the stone.

Devotees left their tributes: a nosegay or a garland or a rose, strewn on the sarcophagus or on the steps approaching it; or fastened to the railings—offerings that were forever renewed, Lamartine said of them, as if by an invisible hand: *éternellement renouvelées sans qu'on voie la main qui les dépose.* Flaubert was sceptical. The sentimentalists who cover the tomb with artificial flowers—are they, he asks, to be allowed to reduce Héloïse to the level of the trivial and silly: *quelque chose de banal et de niais?* They are not required, he continues, to have her knowledge of theology, Greek, or Hebrew, but they could enlarge their hearts, widen their vision, try to appreciate the intelligence and the self-sacrifice manifested in love of such an immensity.

In those early days Père-Lachaise was not like a cemetery, but an unspoilt woodland glade. Paths wound their way under chestnut-trees and limes that in summer flung shadows on meadow-grass bright with flowers. Everything, a contemporary noted, combined to raise the imagination above thoughts of mortality. Then gradually, as one tomb more elaborate than the last crowded upon another, it was transformed into the desolation of tombs that now covers the wooded slopes as far as eye can see: into a city of the dead, laid out in roads and avenues—sign-posts marking the way, vaults and tombs taking the place of houses, a grim *Monument des Morts* presiding like a fortress. Balzac was repelled and attracted by this *Paris microscopique*—a Paris shrunk to the paltry dimensions of death; a place of dust and ashes, where man's sole claim to greatness was his vanity: *un genre humain qui n'a plus rien de grand que sa vanité.*

Graves are packed so close that to look at one is to tread upon another. The old and the new converge, the tombs of the famous and those of the humble. Chopin, Balzac, Sarah Bernhardt, Alfred de Musset, Colette, Oscar Wilde, Ginette Neveu—these rest along with the numberless dead whose names are known, if known at all, only to their kin. Giant slabs of polished marble, the inscriptions upon them newly carved, the dates those of our own times, thrust themselves from among lichen-coated headstones, broken funeral urns, vaults that totter beneath a weight of crumbling masonry. When first I looked at these stones I could not rid myself of the illusion that once they had lived; and then, all in a moment as they jostled to claim right of tenure, were frozen into immobility. The silence is oppressive. Such sounds as there are—the hum of traffic; a footstep on a path; the twitter of a bird; a branch creaking; the clap of a pigeon's wings; leaves fluttering—these are from another world. Here all is touched with unreality—a young man bending over a headstone to decipher an inscription; women shrouded in black standing by a grave where the earth is freshly piled; a cat that pauses, eyes staring, before slipping from view among the tombs. It is a place of death, yet life is stronger than death. In spring cyclamens lift their heads. Buds swell upon the chestnut-trees; bird answers bird in a swelling chorus of song. In summer the sun filters through green, translucent foliage. At the turn of the year holly berries glow red among dark, polished leaves.

It has been said of Héloïse and Abelard that without them the twelfth century would have been dull. So individual, so distinct are their personalities, that they stand apart. It is fitting then, that at Père-Lachaise their grave is not lost among a hundred others. It is in a corner to the south-east, overlooked on one side by tall, quiet houses where at the windows bedding hangs to air or a cat suns itself. It is strange to reflect that there are persons who day in and day out look down at the tomb of Héloïse and Abelard.

The tall houses were the sole reminder of Paris. For the rest I might have been in a country churchyard, where grass had been left to grow, trees to entwine their branches, ivy, moss and lichens to have their way—where one tomb soaring above a clutter of broken gravestones surpasses the rest. It was a day in late autumn. Leaves drifted from a chestnut-tree, making a faint scraping sound as they touched in the air or came to rest on others already fallen. The leaves were a flaming gold, their brightness intensified by sunlight and an unclouded sky. Beneath the Gothic canopy the figures carved in stone that had weathered to an iron-grey darkness rested side by side: lover and beloved; husband and wife; monk and nun—at one in death as they had been in life in the intensity of their suffering and the healing of their suffering. Each had been necessary to the other—to the welfare, the comfort, the redemption of the other. They can no more be separated than in a melody can treble from bass, bass from treble.

Each has conferred immortality upon the other. The nine-teenth-century romantic was right in saying that Héloïse in loving Abelard bestowed upon him an immortal glory: *C'est l'amour d'Héloïse qui fait sa gloire immortelle*. For how many persons today other than specialists in philosophy or mediaeval history would give thought to Abelard were it not that Héloïse had loved him? And he in his turn has bestowed immortality on her. For it is not primarily for her learning that she is remembered, but for her love of Abelard. Had there been no Abelard, posterity would not have known the greatness of Héloïse. Each has attained to glory. If the glory of Héloïse shines the brighter it is because her generosity was the greater. Yet that is not to say that Abelard did not love Héloïse. He loved in his way, she in hers.

These were my thoughts as I came away from the tomb in Père-Lachaise, treading between the gravestones, the golden leaves floating on the stillness of the air. I thought of the legend in the Tours Chronicle, telling how, when the body of Héloïse was brought to be laid at her husband's side, Abe-lard reached out his arms to her. It would have accorded better with the pattern of their lives if it had been Héloïse who reached out hers. And yet perhaps the ancient chronicler was right in thinking that, though the time be slow in coming, a selfless love brings its reward.

BIBLIOGRAPHY

In translating from the letters of Héloïse and Abelard I have used the edition published by J. P. Migne in the *Patrologiae Cursus Completus, Series Latina*: Vol. CLXXVIII. *Petri Abaelardi Abbatis Rugensis Opera Omnia*. Paris 1855.

I am also particularly indebted to the following:

Belloc, Hilaire, *Paris*, London 1912.

Cousin, Victor, *Petri Abaelardi Opera*, Paris 1849.

Gilson, Etienne, *Héloïse et Abélard*, Paris 1948.

Gilson, Etienne, *Héloïse and Abelard*, U.S.A. and Canada 1960.

Haskins, C. H., *The Renaissance in the Twelfth Century*, Camb., Mass. 1927.

Jouhandeau, Marcel, *Lettres d'Héloïse et d'Abélard*, Paris 1959.

Knowles, David, *The Evolution of Medieval Thought*, London 1962.

Leclercq, Jean, *Pierre le Vénérable*, Saint-Wandrille 1946.

McCloud, Enid, *Héloïse*, London 1938.

Muckle, J. T., *Historia Calamitatum, Mediaeval Studies*, Vol. XII (1950), Pontifical Institute, Toronto.

Muckle, J. T., *The Story of Abelard's Adversities* (Translation of above), Toronto 1954.

Poole, Lane, *Illustrations of the History of Medieval Thought and Learning*, London 1960.

Rémusat, Charles de, *Abélard*, Paris 1845.

Stouff, *Héloïse et Abélard: Lettres*, Paris 1964.

Waddell, Helen, *Mediaeval Latin Lyrics*, London 1929.

Waddell, Helen, *The Wandering Scholars*, London 1927.

NOTES

Abbreviation. P.L.: *Patrologia Cursus Completus, Series Latina*

CHAPTER I

1. *Historia Calamitatum* (The Story of Abelard's Adversities)
   This is the title by which Abelard's work is commonly known. Petrarch knew it as such. Another title is *Abaelardi ad Amicum Suum Consolatoria Epistola* (Abelard's Letter of Consolation to a Friend). See J. T. Muckle, *Mediaeval Studies*, Vol. xII, p. 163.

2. *Nominalism: Realism: Universals*
   For the significance of these terms, and the philosophical background of the period see: David Knowles, *The Evolution of Medieval Thought*, and F. Copleston, *History of Philosophy*, Vol. II, London 1952.

CHAPTER II

3. *Schola* can mean an intellectual discipline or a place of teaching. Abelard often uses it in the plural, somewhat loosely, to mean sometimes a course of lectures, sometimes the place in which this is given. See: J. T. Muckle, *Mediaeval Studies*, Vol. xII (1950), p. 176, note 15. For the different kinds of schools (cathedral, monastic and those of individual masters) see: David Knowles, *The Evolution of Medieval Thought*, Ch. vII.

4. *Minor Orders*
   Major Orders are Priest, Deacon, Subdeacon; Minor Orders are Acolyte, Exorcist, Reader, Doorkeeper. The first evidence of all these Orders existing together is found in Pope St. Cornelius (A.D. 251), who enumerates them in his *Epistle to Fabius* (Eusebius *Historia Ecclesiastica*, L. VI, cap. 43). Some of these are much older than the period of St. Cornelius. St. Justin Martyr (110–165) speaks of the Order of Reader (Lector).

5. *Canon*
   The significance of the word in relation to Abelard is discussed by Gilson in *Héloïse and Abelard*, p. 15.

6. *Suscipe Flos Florem*
   This poem is beautifully translated by Helen Waddell:

   > Take thou this rose, O Rose
   > Since Love's own flower it is . . .

   Mediaeval Latin Lyrics, Penguin, p. 264.
   For Abelard's lyrics and his *Planctus* see: Helen Waddell, *Mediaeval Latin Lyrics* (Biographical Notes, pp. 336–337); Raby, *Secular Latin, Poetry*, Vol. II, Oxford 1957. Gilson, *La Théologie Mystique de Saint Bernard*, Appendix II, Paris 1947.

Since handing in my manuscript a most enlightening talk has been given on the Third Programme (Sat. September 16th, 1965, at 9.20 p.m.) on Abelard's *Planctus virginum Israel* by Dr. Peter Dronke, Lecturer in Mediaeval Literature at Cambridge.

CHAPTER III

7. *Philosophers are not Rich*
   This seems a contradiction of Abelard's statement that he was rich. But Héloïse is stating a general truth. The eleventh century had seen the rise of the professional teacher or master who moved from school to school or set up his own school. These, like the Sophists of ancient Greece, accepted fees, and consequently *some* were rich.

8. *Saint Jerome*
   Saint Jerome's deplorable attitude to marriage was derived largely from pre-Christian sources, supported by his own interpretation of Saint Paul. His influence is an example of what happens when the admiration due to a man on one score (in his case scholarship) is extended, without warrant, to other aspects of his thought. Saint John of the Cross realised this danger when he warned that one should take as a model no one (except Christ) however holy, *por santo que sea*, since the devil, he says, will make one admire such a person for the wrong reasons. *San Juan de la Cruz, Obras Completas*, P. José Vicente, C.D., Madrid 1957, p. 77.

CHAPTER IV

9. *He Flung them out*
   This incident is dealt with in detail in Enid McCloud's *Héloïse*, Chatto 1938. There is no slur on the reputation of Héloïse.

CHAPTER V

10. *The Correspondence*
    The authenticity of the Correspondence, which has been questioned in the past, is now established beyond all reasonable doubt. See: Gilson, *Héloïse and Abelard*, Appendix, pp. 145–166.

CHAPTER VI

11. *Woe to the Women . . .* (Ezekiel xiii, 18)
    This is the translation in the Authorised Version. The verse deals with the raising of false hopes by diviners. Ronald Knox who says "the passage remains hopelessly obscure" suggests (in a footnote to his translation of the Old Testament) that it refers to "magical contrivances", and that perhaps "the enquirer slept on pillows stuffed with magical herbs, etc. and took omens from his dreams". He compares Virgil, *Aeneid* VII, 89.

CHAPTER VII

12. *Domino specialiter, sua singulariter*

In the translation of this superscription of Héloïse, I have followed Charles de Rémusat—also Etienne Gilson who says the sense would have been "perfectly clear to her professor of logic". (*Héloïse and Abelard*, p. 103.) I am unconvinced by Enid McCloud's interpretation (also that of George Moore). See: Enid McCloud, *Héloïse*, p. 168.

13. *Greek and Hebrew*

Abelard would not have committed himself to this statement if it had not been true. But how much Greek and Hebrew Héloïse knew it is impossible to say. The writers of classical Greece appear to have been known at this period almost entirely through Latin versions; and this applies also to the Greek Fathers. According to a writer of the seventeenth century Divine Office used to be celebrated in Greek at the Paraclete on the feast of Pentecost. Moreover in the following century there was said to exist in the abbey a thirteenth-century missal containing the Mass in Greek, but written in Roman letters. (See Enid McCloud, *Héloïse*, pp. 182–183.)

As to Hebrew, there were Jewish scholars in France. Sigebert of Gembloux (1030–1112), master of the schools of Metz, used to talk to the Jews on the subject of Saint Jerome's translation of the Hebrew Scriptures.

CHAPTER VIII

14. *Supersubstantialem*

In the Greek of both Matthew and Luke the word is ἐπιούσιον. Possibly *supersubstantialem* (which is a gloss rather than a translation) has reference to the Eucharist. See Ronald Knox's note on this verse in his *New Testament*.

This word appears in the Latin version of the Lord's Prayer that is on the wall of the *Pater Noster* church on the Mount of Olives.

15. *A Frenchman and a monk of Cluny*

The inscription, which is attributed to Peter the Venerable, runs as follows:

> *Hic primo iacuit Petrus Abelardus*
> *Francus et monachus Cluniacensis qui obit anno 1142*
> *Nunc apud moniales Paraclitenses in territoria*
>   *Tricascensi requiscit*
> *Vir pietate insignis scriptis clarissimus*
> *Ingenii acumine rationu pondere dicendi arte*
> *Omni scientiarum genere nulli secundae.*

[Here at first lay Peter Abelard, a Frenchman and a monk of Cluny, who died in the year 1142. Now he rests with the nuns of the Paraclete in the district of Troyes. A man known for his piety, he won special renown for his writings, the sharpness of his intellect, the weight of his reasoning, and his skill as a speaker. In every branch of knowledge he was second to none.]

CHAPTER IX

16. *The bodies of the founder and the first abbess*
Enid McCloud (*Héloïse*, Appendix I) gives the macabre story of the many exhumations and removals of the bones of Héloïse and Abelard, and the preservation of "relics" in Lenoir's Musée des Monuments Français.

CHAPTER X

17. *Breadth of vision*
Unless, and until, more writings of Héloïse come to light she must remain to some degree a mystery. Precisely because there is relatively little to go on, there is perhaps the greater danger of attaching too much weight to what she says in two letters as set against her life of over forty years as a religious. Apposite to the question of fidelity to duty is the following from an article by P. Gabriel de Ste. Marie-Madeleine on *vértu héroïque: l'héroïcité consiste: dans le seul fidèle et constant accomplissement des devoirs et offices personels de chacun* (*Normes Actuelles de la Sainteté. Trouble et Lumière. Etudes Carmelitaines.* Desclée de Brouwer. 1949).

As to her insistence that she did nothing for the love of God, Héloïse appears to think that to love God means to love him in the manner in which she loved Abelard. Abelard's well-intentioned and sometimes moving exhortations that she should love God more than himself would be likely only to confirm her in such a view. Saint John of the Cross (four centuries later) would have found a place for her dilemma in his teaching on the *Noche Oscura.* Religious thought of the twelfth century was concerned less with the problems of the individual soul than with philosophical and theological abstractions. Spiritual direction, as such, was virtually unknown.

CHAPTER XI

18. The Inscription placed by Catherine de La Rochefoucauld under the statue of the Trinity at the Paraclete
Pierre Abailard fondateur de cette abbaye vivoit dans la douzième siècle. Il se distingua par la profondeur de son scavoir et par la rareté de son mérite cependant il publia un traité de la trinite qui fut condamné par un concile tenu à Soissons en 1120. Il se retracta aussitôt par une soumission parfaite et pour témoigner qu'il n'avoit que des sentimens orthodoxes il fit faire de cette seule pierre ces trois figures qui représentent les trois personnes divines dans une nature, après avoir consacré cette église au saint esprit qu'il nomma Paraclet par rapport aux con-

solations qu'il avoit goûtées pendant la retraite qu'il fit en ce lieu. Il avoit épousé Héloyse qui en fut la première abbesse. L'amour qui avoit uni leurs esprits durant leur vie et qui se conserva pendant leur absence par des lettres les plus tendres et les plus spirituelles a réuni leur corps dans ce tombeau. Il mourut le 21 avril l'an 1143, à âgé de 63 ans, après avoir donné l'un et l'autre des marques d'une vie chrétienne et spirituelle.

> *Par très haute et très puissante dame*
> *Catherine de La Rochefoucauld Abbesse.*
> *Le 3 Juin 1701*

N.B.—The date of Abelard's death is incorrect by one year.

CHRONOLOGY

	Abelard	Héloïse	Contemporary French History	Popes	General Contemporary History
1070			William of Champeaux born.		
1073				Gregory VII (Hildebrand) Pope.	
1079	Abelard born, Le Pallet, Brittany.				
1081			Suger born, Argenteuil.		Domesday Book.
1086				Victor III Pope.	William the Conqueror dies.
1087					William II (Rufus) succeeds.
1088					Bayeux tapestry. (?1088)
1091			Bernard of Clairvaux born.		
1093			Peter the Venerable born.		
1096					Durham Cathedral (1130). 1st Crusade (1099).
1099				Pascal II Pope.	Christian Kingdom of Jerusalem. William Rufus killed. Henry I succeeds.
1100	Paris: Dialectic. Abelard disputes teaching of William of Champeaux.	Héloïse born (?1100–1).			

1101		
1102	Abelard's school: (1) at Melun. (2) at Corbeil. Abelard returns to Le Pallet.	
1105		
1108		Louis VI King. William of Champeaux retires to Saint-Victor.
1111	Saint-Victor: Rhetoric. Abelard defeats William of Champeaux in argument. Paris: William's successor abdicates to Abelard.	
1112	William nominates third party master at Notre-Dame. Abelard moves school: (1) to Melun. (2) to Mt. Sainte-Geneviève. Abelard *de facto* Master at Paris. Abelard returns to Le Pallet: His mother enters religion.	Bernard founds Clairvaux. William of Champeaux returns to Paris.

	Abelard	Héloïse	Contemporary French History	Popes	General Contemporary History
1113	Laon: Theology. Abelard's own lectures forbidden by Anselm. Paris: Abelard undisputed Master in Philosophy and Theology.		William of Champeaux Bishop of Châlons.		Thomas à Becket born.
1116	Abelard in House of Fulbert. Tutor to Héloïse.				
1117		Héloïse goes to Le Pallet. Astralabe born.	Abbey of Cluny completed.		
1118		Héloïse goes to Argenteuil.		Gelasius II Pope.	
1119	Paris: Secret marriage of Abelard and Héloïse. Castration of Abelard. Abelard enters religion at Saint-Denis.	Héloïse enters religion at Argenteuil.		Calixtus II Pope.	
1120	Abelard teaches theology at Maisoncelle Priory. *De unitate et trinitate divina.*				
1121	Council of Soissons. Abelard condemned. He burns treatise.		Peter the Venerable Abbot of Cluny.		

	Formal custody Saint-Denis. Absconds to Provins.		
1122	Abelard's appeal to Louis VI. Allowed retire nr. Troyes. Teaches.		
1123	Oratory built. The Paraclete: Dedication attacked. Abelard teaches. *Theologia christiana* and *Sic et non.*		
1124		Adam Abbot of Saint-Denis dies. Succeeded by Suger.	Honorius II Pope.
1126	Abelard elected Abbot of Saint-Gildas-de-Rhuys.		
1128	Suger claims Convent at Argenteuil for Saint-Denis. Héloïse and nuns disperse.		
1129	Abelard's gift of Paraclete to Héloïse. Approval of Bishop of Troyes.		
1130		Argenteuil Convent restored to Saint-Denis.	Innocent II Pope.
1131	Abelard meets Innocent II nr. Etampes. Gift of Paraclete ratified.	Héloïse installed at Paraclete by Abelard.	

	Abelard	Héloïse	Contemporary French History	Popes	General Contemporary History
1132	Saint-Gildas. Attempts on Abelard's life. *Historia Calamitatum.*				
1135	Mt. Sainte-Geneviève. Abelard teaching. John of Salisbury (1115–1180) among scholars.	Paraclete: Papal writ of protection and privilege.			Henry I dies. Stephen succeeds.
1137			Louis VII King.		
1138		Héloïse designated Abbess by Bull of Innocent II.			
1139	William of Saint-Thierry (pupil of Clairvaux) alleges heresy in Abelard's *Introductio ad theologiam.*		Bernard denounces way of life at Cluny.		
1141	Council of Sens. Abelard condemned. Bernard writes to Rome. Abelard's *Apologia* to Héloïse. Abelard sets out for Rome. Learns of papal condemnation: withdraws to Cluny.				

Year	Abelard & Paraclete	France & Arts	Crusade / England	Popes & Prelates
1142	Abelard dies at Saint-Marcel, nr. Chalon-sur-Saône. Peter the Venerable writes to Héloïse. Peter the Venerable brings body of Abelard to Paraclete.			
1143				Celestine II (scholar of Abelard) Pope.
1144		Saint-Denis: Gothic choir and stained glass of Suger.		Lucius II Pope.
1145		Bernard preaches 2nd crusade.		Eugenius III Pope.
1146				
1148		Suger Regent of France.	2nd crusade fails at Damascus.	
1151		Suger dies.		
1153				Anastasius IV Pope.
1154			Stephen dies. Henry II succeeds.	Adrian IV (Breakspear) Pope.
1159				Alexander III Pope.
1162				Becket Archbishop.
1163				
1164	Paraclete: Héloïse dies. Buried with Abelard.	Notre-Dame de Paris (1260).		

INDEX

BRITTANY

vannes

st. gildas-de-rhuys

nantes

le pal

clisson

Abelard

Héloïse

palace

notre-dame

Fulbert's house

mount ste. geneviève

abbey of st. victor

PARIS

12th-Century FRANCE